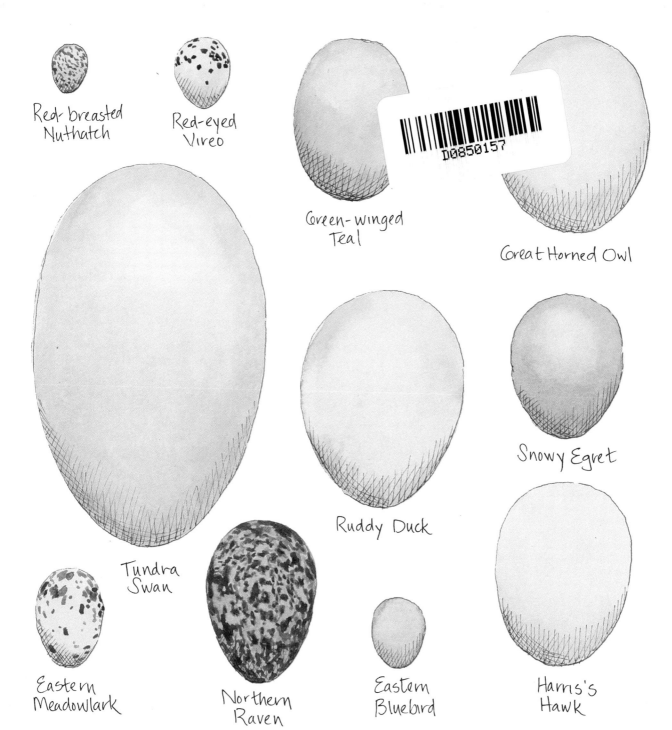

Red-breasted Nuthatch

Red-eyed Vireo

Green-winged Teal

Great Horned Owl

Tundra Swan

Ruddy Duck

Snowy Egret

Eastern Meadowlark

Northern Raven

Eastern Bluebird

Harris's Hawk

D0850157

SECRETS
OF THE NEST

The Family Life of North American Birds

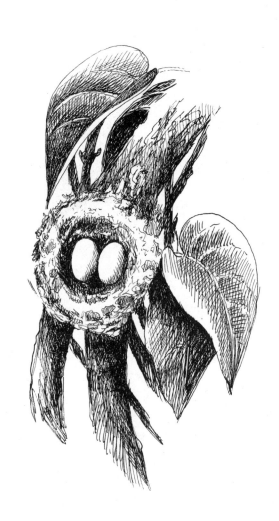

SECRETS OF THE NEST

~

The Family Life of
North American Birds

Written and illustrated by
JOAN DUNNING

Houghton Mifflin Company
BOSTON   NEW YORK   1994

For information about permission to reproduce selections
from this book, write to Permissions, 215 Park Avenue South,
New York, NY 10003

Library of Congress Cataloging-in-Publication Data
Dunning, Joan
Secrets of the nest : The family life of North American birds /
written and illustrated by Joan Dunning.
p.   cm.
ISBN 0-395-62035-X
1. Birds — North America — Nests. 2. Birds — North America — Eggs.
3. Birds — North America.   I. Title.
QL675.D8   1994
598.256'4'097 — dc20   93-32569
                                        CIP

Printed in the United States of America

MP 10 9 8 7 6 5 4 3 2 1

Book design by Melodie Wertelet

The author is grateful for permission to reprint material from *The Trees,* by Conrad
Richter, copyright © 1940, renewed 1968 by Conrad Richter. Reprinted by permission
of Alfred A. Knopf, Inc.

John Muir's essay "The Water Ouzel" originally appeared in *The Mountains of
California,* copyright © 1916 by John Muir, Houghton Mifflin Company.

Acknowledgments

Several years ago, an editor named Karen Klockner, who worked for a highly regarded children's book publisher, called me out of the blue and said, "I think you have an instinct for writing for children. Would you like to write for us?" She and I talked for a long time about possible topics.

Can one "hear" a "spark" over the phone, 3,000 miles away? Apparently, because she called me back the next day after our long conversation, convinced that she knew what the topic for my next book should be.

"Chaparral?" I asked. Because I thought that was clearly the topic about which I had been most animated.

"No . . . the nests."

The minute she said this, I had a feeling that she knew me far better than I knew myself. Yes. The nests. I had a sensation of going home. "Yes." And this book was conceived.

It did not remain a children's book, however. It grew up. One night, lying in a small tent out on the "Lost Coast" south of here, I realized that I was struggling too hard to contain my thoughts in words for children. I resolved to abandon a year's work, switch publishers (I was not yet under contract) and lope along in a voice that suited my adult stride.

But this new form was far more demanding in the long run. Thank you to Don Allen, Larry Eifert, Mary Glendinning, Jake Drake, and Kathleen Leonardi for reading and advising me from this coast. And thank you to my delightful editors at Houghton Mifflin Co., Harry Foster and Susan Kunhardt, for further molding the book into shape. Finally, thank you to Ron Le Valley for reading it for accuracy.

JOAN DUNNING
Ferndale, California

For Suzanne and David,
who have been so patient with the slow evolution
of this book. That they both still love to write and both
still love nests is rather a mystery to me.

Contents

List of Color Illustrations

In the robin's nest there were Eggs. . . . in the garden there was nothing which did not understand the wonderfulness of what was happening — the immense, tender, terrible, heart-breaking beauty and solemnity of Eggs. If there had been one person in that garden who had not known through all his or her innermost being that if an Egg were taken away or hurt the whole world would whirl round and crash through space and come to an end . . . there could have been no happiness even in that golden springtime air.

— from *The Secret Garden,*
FRANCES HODGSON BURNETT

Introduction

~

About 25 years ago, I began to realize that, in my future, nature might not remain a buxom goddess but was perhaps taking on the qualities of a tired and mortal old man leaning on a staff. At that time, however, I found a place of refuge from my growing sense of global doom, and it was there that I did a drawing that is the origin of this book. In fact, I think that this book has grown out of a desire to return to that place, to be enveloped once again by its walls, to be numbed by the focus I enjoyed as I did that drawing long ago.

Up in the foothills of Santa Barbara, near the old Spanish mission, under ancient dark oaks that once shaded Indians and missionaries, there is a natural history museum. I remember a sense of leaving the mortal world behind whenever I passed into the protection of its thick adobe walls. There seemed no need to speak to the person at the front desk; I simply faded into the cool, still interior, turned left around a sunny little courtyard, followed a narrow hallway until I reached an odd little switchback doorway through which I passed into a dim and ageless

room. A stuffed condor flew overhead. In this room nothing became extinct. For me, beneath the condor's gaze, a California of 200 years ago stretched out in repose, timeless, free of housing tracts and roads. Rising on a thermal, wheeling and eyeing the land below for something dead or dying, the condor soared on giant wings while its naked pink and yellow head angled down in perpetual observation. I used to enter this room and pause in relief. Here the Earth would not die.

All around the walls of the room in lighted showcases there were colorful stuffed birds, but it was to the old, heavy, free-standing glass-topped cases in the center of the room that I was drawn. Inside were countless nests, and within each nest there were eggs. I was perhaps 19 at the time, well into breeding age myself. Very likely my interest was intensified by my own biological readiness to bear young. But the smooth form of an egg has lost none of its power to fascinate and soothe me, now that I have had children and approach the end of breeding age.

When I first started going to the egg room, as I called it, I had not consciously acknowledged to myself that I actually "liked birds." In fact, I was amused and a little puzzled by the bird watchers that I met in the marsh near the university, particularly one man who always carried a rather phallic-looking scope wrapped with plastic vines. I was not raised to like birds. I was raised to like plants. People in my family, when they looked up, looked at trees. To begin to like birds would be like changing religions.

I still have the drawing, old and yellowed, that triggered this conversion. It was of a cormorant nest. I have often thought of cormorants as looking more functional than beautiful. They hold their beaks upward as if they are anxious, dive quickly, and surface furtively. Their grace is fleeting, if not nonexistent. Predictably, cormorants do not build particularly beautiful nests.

Instead, they throw together careless piles of sticks and seaweed littered with guano, dead fish, and even dead chicks. Their eggs, which are a delicate blue-white when laid, are stained brown with the guano of the adults as incubation progresses. Of course, the nest I drew was a neat museum reassembly designed not to rot; a pile of clean sticks and seaweed with a hollow containing the eggs.

I believe I chose the cormorant nest almost at random, out of a general desire to draw any nest at all. The drawing is important to me not because of its subject matter but because of the feeling it evoked. As I drew, weaving sticks and seaweed on paper, there gradually developed a rhythm to the motion of my pencil that felt birdlike. The repetitious laying on of material grew pleasantly mindless, instinctive, abstract. For an hour or two, I was a bird.

And then I drew the eggs.

The double-crested cormorant builds a platform nest of sticks on the ground or in trees, usually in colonies, always near water. Nest types are not mixed in a colony; all of the nests are either in trees or on the ground.

Defining the oval shapes with my pencil, my hand moved in smooth arcs around these strange, otherworldly, inscrutable objects. As I drew, a calm came over me like the calm that comes over an incubating bird after the activity of courtship and nest-building. The eggs were so perfect, so self-sufficient, so complete. As often happens when I draw from nature, I saw not only the form but the miracle of what I drew.

As I continued drawing, however, I realized that the eggs also evoked in me a strange, incongruous feeling of unease. How could the two go together, calm and unease? Then I realized that, of course, while an incubating bird might have to be calm in order to steadily warm eggs, it does not necessarily feel calm. While an egg may look perfect, the world into which it is laid offers far from perfect conditions for its survival. This mix of calm and anxiety matched my feelings about nature in general. I experienced the eggs as microcosms of all that is perfect, all that is vulnerable and, most importantly, all that is inherently unknown about our Earth. Like an astronaut finally flying far enough out to pause in space and contemplate this little egg we live on, I saw eggs. I looked right and left in the showcase at nest after nest, and in each one, there they were! Even more remarkable, the eggs were not all the same, not generic performers of miracles; they were all different! Some were tiny, some huge; some pointed, some almost completely round; some white, some brown, some blue, some speckled. Clearly each nestful had a different story to tell. I was hooked.

* * *

A few years ago a retired school librarian described to me her years of watching children check out books. She said she noticed that about half the children were eager to lay their hands on "nature books," while the others checked out fiction. The next week,

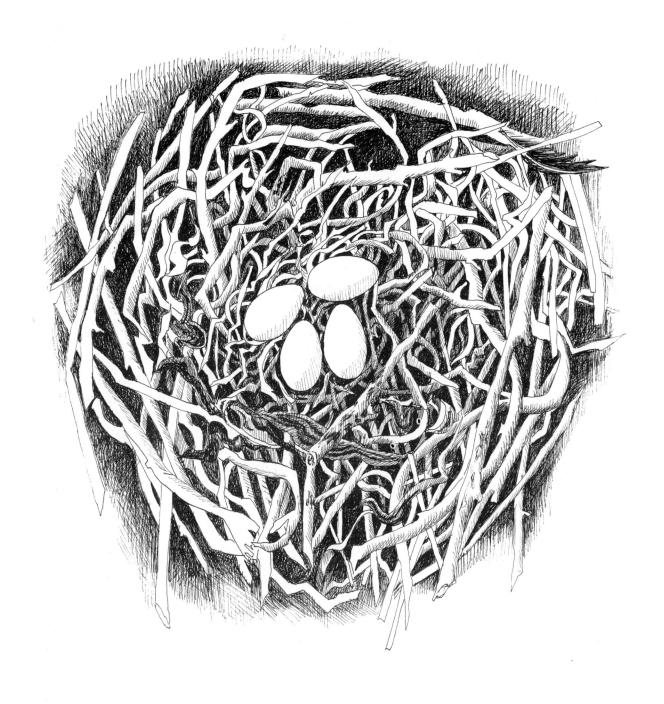

when the books came back, the children with the fiction chattered excitedly about what they had read, while the others had little to say. She was genuinely troubled, for she felt that a need was not being met. Upon investigation she found that there was no one at home helping to bring to life the more inert pages of the nonfiction books.

Most education leaves adults remarkably ignorant of the natural world. Even college graduates often know little more than their kids do. Those questions that children ask — "What are the slugs doing all curled up with each other like that?" or "Why do the earthworms drown in the puddles when it rains?" or "Which whales have teeth?" — bring us up short. In the absence of knowledge, however, we can share our curiosity. We can set an example that learning about nature is an endeavor to enrich a lifetime.

Several years ago I was asked to speak to a large conference on environmental education. As I prepared my talk, trying to imagine what the audience needed to know that would help them inspire and excite children to learn about nature, I wound up analyzing how I had picked up my own passion for the natural world. I felt that people were at that conference to become better wizards, better magicians, to compete with television and Nintendo. But how is a passion for nature instilled in a child? I came to the conclusion, as I examined my past, that it is often through the example of an adult who does not simply, dutifully teach about nature "for the children's sake," but who is selfishly, personally passionate about nature for his or her own sake.

I grew up in the Los Angeles basin, a dry land now irrigated, where remnants of the orange groves that replaced the savanna still exist here and there in back yards. The smog climbed the face of the San Gabriel Mountains during my childhood, killing on its way up what trees existed among the chaparral. I used to

look down from the front summit of that steep and crumbling range and ache for my birthright. Surely I was meant to have clean air to breathe. My father hated the smog, the tameness of our neighborhood. I remember midnight wake-ups: "We're leaving for the desert now. I can't sleep." It was a strange childhood. In winter, on weekends, we went to the Mojave, setting up camp in rather fantastic places with Dr. Seusslike joshua trees and eerily spired dry washes carved by flash floods. We rarely took a tent. We just put our sleeping bags out on the ground, and my father, who was rather lizardlike, sat in a webbed chair in the sun, with his skinny legs crossed, reading and smoking cigarettes. Our little table and Coleman stove seemed like such a tiny stake on existence out there in the wide desert. The stars would come out and surround us, and coyotes would arrive to sniff us in our beds.

But what made these and other trips magical was when my father would start exploring. I remember setting up wars with him between red and black ants, having to scurry around looking for replacement troops; or dropping insects into doodlebug pits so we could see the victims buried alive; or looking through a magnifying glass at dewy green cicadas that had just shed their skins; or sitting up with him in the darkness to watch the nocturnal animals come out so we could photograph them. He did not watch nature to teach us. I felt he would have been doing all of these things anyway, even if we weren't along.

Now, this was not a model childhood. My father was a mild-mannered alcoholic, subject to bouts of dazed introspection, a sort of depressed high priest of nature. Nevertheless, my brother and I were deeply and permanently affected by his absorption in the natural world. For me, those childhood experiences made a god of the cicada, a mint green scarab that lives at the core of my soul. In childhood, we look to the adults we deeply love, however imperfect they may be, for our myths. What shall our children's gods be?

As I have worked on this book, some people whom I have told about it have assumed that I am writing for children. While this book is intended primarily for adults, I hope that it will be read on several levels and its facts and concepts shared with young people. I don't mean to imply that this book must be read with a child on one's lap. But I worry that not only TV, but the chain link fence and the rubber ball are replacing the pursuits of all those days children used to spend prowling the woods. The art of setting up ant wars and hermit crab races is being lost. The art of looking, just to see what's there, is being abandoned. Our planet can't afford this ignorance.

These days I see fewer and fewer birds. In early winter, after a heavy rain, I go to check whether the tundra swans have returned to the delta near my home. If there are no swans, I am not satisfied just to breathe the fresh air coming in off the ocean. I'm impatient for proof that the swans have had a safe breeding season. When they do finally return, long-necked and white, gracing our valley's flooded pastures, I take my children's friends with us to see them, so that we will all speak a similar language, so that we will all know, as one, the significance of swans.

*   *   *

This book is not intended to be a field guide. There already exist several excellent field guides to the birds' nests of the United States. It is my intention that this book will make using those field guides more meaningful and enjoyable. Nest identification down to the species level is often very difficult. What I find exciting are the broader concepts that explain the existence of such a tremendous variety of nests and eggs and nesting habits. I hope to simplify and bring these to life for you.

It has been very difficult to decide which species to include in this book. Certain species have come and gone repeatedly from my list, for various reasons. My choices are based on many criteria. First of all, I have tried to choose classic examples of the various types of nests — ground, platform, burrow, cavity, cup, pendulous. Then I have included interesting variations on these forms. I have also included many birds that have some unusual breeding habits, for example, the Harris's hawk, which often nests cooperatively. I have included birds that I happen to love for one reason or another, however personal. I might have included a bird, for instance, simply because on some forgotten evening the air smelled of sage as I stood, binoculars in hand, watching it. And, finally, I have included some birds for no other reason than that there are certain irascible people out there who would get mad at me if their favorite birds were left out.

There are a lot of beautiful and amazing birds. Instead of my job getting easier as I have gone along, because I might have become willing to jettison species the way a tired hiker jettisons belongings from a heavy pack, I have squeaked, "Just one more?" and let another in. At the same time, I have tried to keep this book simple. Please realize that I have only been thinking of my reader when I have gotten tough with myself and regretfully opened the book to let a bird fly from these pages.

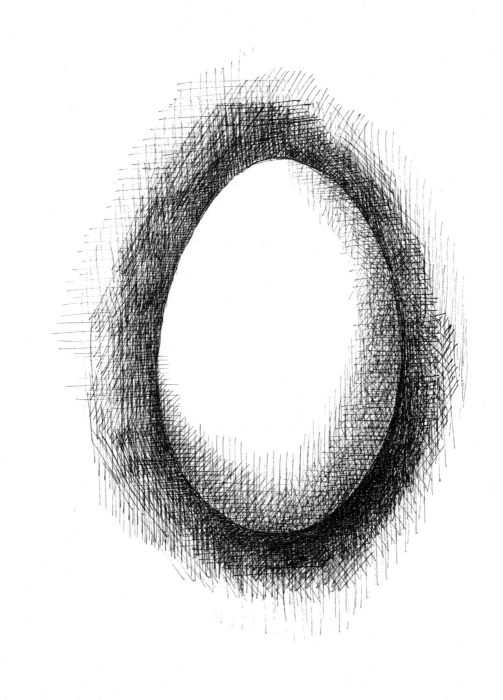

1
Eggs

~

It is easy to take eggs for granted. Each day parents all around the country stand half awake in their kitchens, holding a cup of coffee in one hand and an egg in the other as they sleepily ask their children, "Want cereal or eggs?" "Eggs, I guess." "Scrambled or fried?" "Fried." "One or two?" "One." Parents ask, children answer. An egg is an egg.

But the whole subject of nests gets rather suspenseful when you realize a few simple facts of bird life. The first one is: *Eggs roll.* They not only roll, but they *break.* I don't know how tender the maternal or paternal instincts of a bird are, but I know how I would feel if one of my children were in there.

The suspense is compounded when you realize another fact: *Birds don't have hands.* This sounds obvious, but think about it. We have this funny little animal walking or hopping along on two feet, with its hands essentially tied behind its back, the survival of its species dependent on how well it can protect and keep warm a ridiculous, round, rolly, fragile thing containing its future offspring.

I tried it. I put an egg on my kitchen floor and got down on my knees and held my hands behind my back, and pushed the egg with my nose. I heard foxes in the living room, snakes in the broom closet, and raccoons sneaking around in the cabinets behind the cereal boxes. And then I thought, this isn't for just a morning, this could be for two weeks, three weeks, a month! And imagine taking care of not just one of these round rolly things, but five or six, out on a branch, 20 feet off the ground! How did this whole rather absurd situation come about, these birds caring for eggs in high, dangerous places?

If you look in a chicken's cold, beady little eye and say the word "lizard," you will almost instantly see, beneath all those soft and polite feathers, a reptile in disguise. Millions of years ago, the scales of some of the smaller, upright dinosaurs grew feathery for warmth. Over more millions of years these fast little dinosaurs began to use their feathery "arms" to lift themselves into the air. Gradually, lightweight bones were favored and powerful flight muscles developed, and we had birds.

But, unlike present-day reptiles, birds evolved from warm-blooded dinosaurs called the coelurosaurs. Warm-bloodedness requires that greater attention be paid to the once simple act of reproduction. A cold-blooded reptile like a turtle can lay its eggs in a hole, bury them, and go on its way. But the eggs of warm-blooded animals must be kept warm until they are mature enough to hatch. But how?

If the eggs are to be buried, then there must be some sort of heat available. One group of birds, the megapodes, which live in the South Pacific, employ the heat of the sun, rotting vegetation, or even volcanic activity to do the job. Best known of the megapodes is the mallee fowl of southern Australia, the male of which spends most of each year creating and maintaining a huge nest 15 feet in diameter. This mound is built over a large hole that the bird digs and fills with leaves and then covers with a deep layer of sand. Once his mate has laid her eggs inside the mound, the male monitors the nest, testing the internal temperature by pulling out beakfuls and using his tongue as a thermometer. For eight weeks, one of the longest incubation periods of any species of bird, he works to keep the nest temperature constant, pulling off the leaves and sand by day and replacing them at night. When the chicks are finally ready to hatch, the mallee fowl and his mate, as if exhausted by the whole long and complicated process, completely abandon them to hatch on their own in an abrupt reversion to a more typically reptilian style.

Archaeopteryx, which lived 140 million years ago, was probably one of the links between reptiles and birds. Its sharp teeth, long, bony tail, and three clawed fingers on each forelimb are almost disturbingly reptilian on a creature with feathers and wings.

Mammals flourished in the period that followed the demise of the dinosaurs. This fact had a significant impact on the evolution of birds, favoring birds that built their nests in high, out-of-the-way locations. The opossum, the most primitive mammal in North America, has managed to survive since the Cretaceous Period, over 65 million years ago.

Among most other species of birds alive on Earth today, there has evolved an improved method of incubation — the use of the body heat of one or both of the parents. In its most primitive form, this is accomplished by the female simply scraping out a slight hollow in the ground to keep her eggs from rolling and then plunking herself down on top of them until they hatch. Of course there is risk involved with this simple approach. Following the demise of the giant dinosaurs 65 million years ago, not only the birds but two other groups of animals, the mammals and insects, flourished and eventually shared domination of the Earth. Of particular danger to birds were the mammals, which began as an insignificant population of small and shrewlike little creatures but multiplied, growing steadily larger and more clever. Eggs, chicks, and the parents themselves all became increasingly vulnerable to attack.

Fortunately for all who love the wide variety of birds existing today, warm-bloodedness, combined with feathers for insulation and wings for flight, made birds highly adaptive contenders for niches left empty by the giant dinosaurs plus many other niches that reptiles had never attempted to colonize. These environments often provided greater safety from predators and minimal competition for food. As birds adapted to the demands and opportunities of these new environments, new species evolved. Not only did these species look different in each different habitat, but they evolved new and varied behaviors, including how they nested and cared for their young.

And so we come to the subject of this book. If I were pressed to give it in a single word, it would be "variety" — variety of habitats, variety of adaptations, the delightful forking that has occurred as the evolution of birds has flowed around environmental obstacles and responded to environmental opportunities. What is exciting is that there are birds still nesting virtually as they did at each stage of evolutionary development. As a result, we have a traceable living record of evolution in the incredible variety of nests that are built on Earth today.

Of course, at the center of all of this activity lie the eggs. For all the changes nests have gone through, eggs have actually changed very little. They are the passive receivers of care, inert, defenseless, the sustainers of the life of each species. Their very "helplessness" has seemed to bring out a concomitant "creativity" in the parent birds. I suggest that you try reading this book with your hands clasped behind your back, using only your nose to turn the pages. With this handicap you will remember to appreciate each nest as one further evolutionary answer to the enduring question, "How can I keep my eggs safe?"

2

Natural Selection and the Nest

~

Before we begin looking at individual nests, it is important to have one concept readily at hand, that of natural selection. It is this force of nature that explains the highly various forms of nests. Each form fills certain needs, solves certain problems.

Imagine a marsh. A breath of breeze blows through old dry cattails from last year that stand, sun-bleached and worn, above this year's emerging shoots. Blackbirds perch sideways on the old reeds, angling to defend their mates and their territories with noisy, gurgling calls. It is a welcome, joyous tumult to our human ears — pushy, like spring.

We scan the cattails with binoculars until our eyes catch a hint of movement, and we retrace a bit of shore. In the reeds at the water's edge is a bird, its beak pointed straight up to expose the full length of its striped throat, while its yellow eyes are aimed straight in our direction. The cattails lean slightly in the breeze, and the bird slowly sways back and forth with the reeds. She is an American bittern, shy ground nester of the marsh. Be-

The American bittern builds a platform nest of reeds on the shores of marshes. Her nestlings, if threatened, will throw their beaks skyward just as their mother does, though they lack the brown and white striped plumage necessary to make this defensive gesture effective.

neath her, nestled in her platform of reeds by the shore, there are five olive-buff eggs.

Even a nestful of newly hatched bitterns, pink with skimpy white down on their bodies, will throw their beaks upwards, as if they already had rich brown coloration to help them blend with the reeds. Of course they have not been instructed in this futile activity; it is automatic. It has come about gradually by means of countless instances of survival by those individuals who appear most like the marsh itself, and countless demises of those who remained fatally birdlike.

In bitterns, natural selection has worked to modify coloration and the behavior and physical structure of the adult. Bitterns' eyes actually bulge out when the beak is thrust upward, so the bird can continue to have frontal vision, permitting it to flee at the last moment should cryptic coloration fail. Also, when the adult is absent from the nest, the greenish brown eggs blend with their reed bed.

With natural selection in mind as the mechanism that results in the varying adaptations that permit each species to survive, let's look at the different types of nests that have evolved through time. What makes the study of nesting so interesting is observing the particular set of adaptations that help each species survive this period of vulnerable immobility.

THE GROUND NEST

The earliest birds laid their eggs right on the ground. Many birds still nest this way today. Often, as a part of ritualized courtship display, the female pivots on her breast, pushing with her feet. This results in a slight depression in the sand or soil into which she then deposits her eggs. As we examine some representative ground nesters we will see what defenses have evolved that have enabled species to continue to nest in this very primitive way.

One of the earliest modifications in the evolution of nesting was the introduction of extra vegetative material to the ground nest. Birds that evolved during this stage of development made the revolutionary move of beginning to pull surrounding vegetation toward them with their beaks while on the nest site. This activity, too, probably originated as a chance movement in courtship display or nest exchange. It has persisted because the mounding up of material results in increased safety from water and predators.

THE PLATFORM NEST

One of the next significant evolutionary changes was for birds to begin to deliberately pick up material and carry it in their beaks to the nest. This is very different from the more primitive drawing in of material. To actually choose a stick and walk or fly with it to the nest is a much more "intentional" act, one that opened up a whole new range of possibilities for nest building.

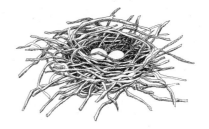

Later, birds began elevating the vegetative material on which they would lay their eggs. This took further "premeditation" since adequate material to support the eggs had to be lodged in the shrub or tree prior to laying. The material in these still relatively primitive nests is not woven or shaped but simply heaped in elevated platforms.

THE BURROW

The burrow may have had its origin with ground nesters that took advantage of the protection of crevices or lived where the soil was particularly penetrable. Using beaks or feet to dig may have been a chance move performed during courtship,

but increasingly deeper scrapes resulted in improved conceal-ment of the eggs. Some species eventually became masterful tunnelers.

THE CAVITY NEST

Other species' chances for survival significantly improved when they began tucking their eggs into preexisting cavities in trees. These cavities sheltered the adults from cold and sun and put them farther out of reach of predators.

Some birds evolved adaptations for chiseling wood that en-abled them to excavate large cavities where none existed before. Once abandoned by their original occupants, these cavities often become the homes of species that do not have the capability of excavating for themselves.

THE CUP NEST

Meanwhile, some birds began to make the platform nest more secure by weaving its vegetative material and even adding sticky binders, resulting in strong, deeply cupped nests. This is the most familiar bird nest, perhaps because, thanks to its weaving and binding, it is the type of nest most easily collected. While it is hard to carry home and proudly display a ground nest or a platform nest or a burrow, beautiful, complete examples of cup nests are brought home by the hundreds.

The cup nest has also found its way into cavities, for the combined security of a warm roof and walls and a cozy "bed" below. It is also built on the ground.

THE PENSILE NEST

As birds have evolved, becoming smaller and more agile, nesting higher and higher up in trees has proved to be one of the most effective ways to avoid predators. Additionally, the farther out on a branch a bird can nest, the more predators it can avoid.

Certain species of midsized song birds, without becoming diminutive in size, have developed specialized techniques for nesting out on the smallest twigs. The pensile nest is actually a tiny hammock suspended between the forks of small twigs that would not support a cup nest of comparable size.

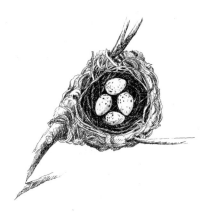

THE PENDULOUS NEST

The final word in arboreal nesting to date is the pendulous nest. Inaccessible even to airborne predators, it is a hanging pouch, able to contain a relatively large bird with relatively large eggs suspended from the tiniest of twigs. Pendulous nests are most common in the tropics, but there are a few admirable examples built by North American birds.

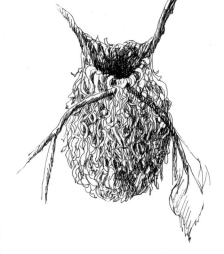

NO NEST

It is not surprising that already a predator should be invading many of the masterful nests built far out on tiny twigs by the one route left open to them, the air. Parasitic birds are those that do not build their own nests but dart into the nests of other birds to lay their eggs. The host parent rears the parasite's young, leaving the latter free to keep laying in other nests.

3

Ground Nests

~

I have a special fondness for ground nests, perhaps because they so completely open up our idea of nests. While some ground nests are lined with vegetation, many are little more than shallow depressions the parent bird makes by pivoting on its breast in sand or gravel. Some species do not alter the surface of the ground at all before laying their eggs.

I like the irony of fragile eggs lying on gravel or sand or even bare rock. I like, too, the fact that the eggs are completely visible. The oval forms in such a spare setting have a look of nature imitating art, as if the eggs themselves might well be made of stone and placed in a raked Zen garden.

I am fascinated by how birds have gotten away with laying their eggs on the ground for so many thousands of years. While we think of the cup as the classic nest form, ground nests are actually far more primitive. Over time, a wide range of adaptations has evolved, compensating for the vulnerability of eggs laid on the ground.

The least tern, like many of the more primitive birds, lays its eggs directly on bare ground. The eggs are contained only by a "scrape," a shallow depression formed by the female as she pivots her breast in sand or gravel.

Terns

Pale sand, some broken pieces of white, chalky clam shell, and the slightest depression to keep the eggs from rolling — that is all there is. The eggs, too, are pale buff, chalky, with brown speckles over their surfaces that blend with bits of seaweed and gravel.

Above our heads, terns wheel and call. In the distance at regular intervals over the beach, more terns rest, upright, incubating eggs. We have stumbled on a colony of least terns. With so many birds in the air and the eggs so effectively camouflaged, it is impossible to tell just how many nests may be in our path. We turn to carefully retrace our steps and leave the birds in peace, when all at once, from out of nowhere, a tern swoops low, actually hitting the top of my head with its beak. Another joins in, calling raucously and attracting more birds. The attack quickly escalates — the birds are not only hitting us with their beaks but dropping excrement on our heads with unnerving accuracy. There is no time to watch our step. We simply run, back the way we came.

It is easy to see how terns, one of the oldest genera of birds in North America, have managed to exist for 50 million years. Relatives of gulls, they are tough fighters. It is only in the last 200 years of their long existence that their numbers have dropped to dangerously low levels over much of their range because of the impact of humans prepared to brave the birds' assaults. In the 1800s the least tern was practically annihilated so that its feathers, wings, and even whole stuffed birds could decorate the brims of women's hats. By 1913, terns were protected and began a comeback, only to have to fight against people and bulldozers seeking beach frontage. In 1969, the Endangered Species Act came to terns' aid, and they are currently making a slight re-

Birds that nest in colonies are often highly synchronized, the whole colony mating at approximately the same time and producing chicks within days of one another. This permits the adults to defend both eggs and young collectively. The least tern, like other terns, dive bombs and rains excrement on intruders.

covery. During the nesting season, some colonies are actually guarded 24 hours a day by concerned individuals and organizations.

One of the most interesting times to watch terns is early in spring, before the birds have paired off and begun incubation. Male birds seeking mates wheel in the air, swooping low over the birds on the ground. As if to demonstrate their ability to provide for their mates, many of the males carry in their beaks small silver fish that glint in the sun. They swoop and rise in displays of pure vitality until the females begin to join in and the birds fly together, fast and high, calling loudly. Out of this frenetic activity, pair bonds gradually form. Two by two, birds rise above the wheeling flock and then swoop down in unison like trick pilots.

Small fish continue to function as the currency of intimacy before and during copulation. On a beach littered with gravel and shells, dried seaweed has blown or been left by tides in small tangled heaps. Dune plants with tap roots sunk deep into the sand for moisture have sent out delicate, bright flowers that are invulnerable to the harsh, salty wind. A female tern lands on the sand. Seconds later, her new mate alights a few feet away, his fish held sideways in his beak. As the male tips his head back and forth, the silvery sides of the dead fish gleam. He may as well have pulled up in an expensive car outfitted with brightly polished chrome. The female flutters her wings excitedly as the two birds circle one another on foot. The male, too, begins fluttering, until finally he comes up behind the female and mounts her back, still holding the fish in his beak. Among birds, copulation generally takes only seconds, since in most species all that is involved is the brief coming together of the cloacas of male and female. At this precise moment of coitus, the female tern tips her head backward, takes the silver fish from the beak of the male, and swallows it.

Least Tern

NEST
Slight depression on bare ground

HABITAT
Ocean beaches, sandbars in rivers, cleared land, even gravel roofs

EGGS
2–3, brown-speckled

INCUBATION
20–21 days, by both parents

BREEDING RANGE
Both coastlines of North America and rivers in the interior of the United States. Winters in South America

As with many colonial birds, the pairs of terns in this colony mate at about the same time. As a result, the eggs are deposited on the warm sand nearly simultaneously. The male and the female take turns incubating, the bird that has been off the nest often returning with fish to feed its mate. At the end of the 20-day incubation period, lively brown speckled chicks begin hatching everywhere. The chicks are semiprecocial. This means that they are hatched covered with warm down, with their eyes open, and are able to walk, run, and even swim. But, unlike true precocial chicks, which are capable of finding their own food soon after hatching, each brood of one to three little terns stays in the vicinity of its nest site, assembling promptly upon a parent's return with food.

Needless to say, the sudden arrival of so many lively chicks throws the colony abruptly into chaos. Tiny chicks dash everywhere. The advantage of the breeding colony is clear, however. While a single pair of terns nesting on the open sand would be no match for a predator, as a mob the terns have a chance of keeping their young safe until they fledge a month and a half later.

The least tern chick is camouflaged to blend with the sand. Even the inside of the eggshell, which might attract attention to the newly hatched chick, is speckled rather than white.

Murres

On the eastern side of a rocky island somewhere off the coast of Greenland or Newfoundland, cliffs rise a thousand feet above crashing surf that pounds in from the open Atlantic. The cliffs are vertical, yet because they are of sedimentary rock, the entire face is notched with irregular ledges where one limestone layer has worn faster than the next. On each of these ledges, anywhere there is a hint of a horizontal surface, upright birds are packed shoulder to shoulder, incubating their eggs.

The birds are murres. They are black and white, and with their vertical posture and reduced wings for underwater locomotion, they look remarkably like small penguins stranded out of their element. In fact, murres are members of the auk family, which is considered to be the Northern Hemisphere's equivalent of the penguin.

Even more striking than the density with which the birds are packed on the cliff is the noise they make. Before there were lighthouses, it was illegal to kill murres off this coast, because the sound of the colonies warned sailors of the presence of islands in the fog. The birds *murr*, hence their name, and purr and growl and moan in what seems like an unnervingly chaotic parody of the stresses of overpopulation. Yet all this noise is what keeps the cliff face in rather remarkable order and harmony. With murres shoulder to shoulder, sometimes in actual bodily contact with one another, each pair still defends its own minuscule territory. To avoid the suggestion of trespass, the intention of nearly every move must be communicated formally in advance. When a murre passes other nests, it moves in a ritualized walk that demonstrates the bird's lack of malice. In spite of this exaggerated attention to communication, squabbles break out continually, brought quickly under control by appeasement displays involving the turning aside of the beak in formalized preening.

The territory of each pair is usually only a couple of square feet, yet year after year the pair return to this same exact bit of rock and fiercely defend it. The male and female of a pair rendezvous in spring after eight months of separation spent in warmer waters to the south. In such limited space, little display is needed to identify one another and rebond. Once each pair's single egg is laid, territories are generally occupied only by the incubating adult. With so many eggs seemingly strewn along the bare cliffs, urgent questions leap to mind. Why don't the eggs roll off? How does a murre recognize its own egg among thousands? How can they risk laying only one? How have murres survived such a seemingly chancy setup?

Actually, murres are one of the most common seabirds in the world. They are unusually long-lived — banded birds have been observed breeding at the age of 20, and it is suspected that they may live much longer than this. Long-lived species of birds can get away with laying fewer eggs, since fewer surviving chicks are needed annually to maintain a stable population. In any case, it seems unlikely that a pair of murres would be capable of caring for more than one egg at a time, not to mention multiple chicks, on a rocky ledge a thousand feet above the ocean! Murre eggs, however, are remarkable among bird eggs for being pronouncedly pyriform, or pear-shaped. This shape causes the egg to roll in an arc when it is accidentally nudged, instead of going straight off the cliff as a round woodpecker egg would.

It has been speculated that recognition of eggs might be aided by the fact that murre eggs come in an exceptional variety of colors and patterns — everything from white to blue, green, brown, and lavender shells, scrawled and dotted with black and lilac and browns. As with all patterned eggs, the speckles and

NEST
On bare rock
HABITAT
Rocky cliffs of offshore islands
EGGS
1 large, pointed egg in any of a variety of colors
INCUBATION
32–33 days, by both parents
BREEDING RANGE
Along the northern Atlantic Coast of North America, and the Pacific Coast as far south as central California

Murres often lay their eggs on ledges little more than a foot wide, hundreds of feet above crashing surf. A chicken egg would roll right off. The murre egg is exceptionally pointed, however, and rolls in a circle if bumped.

scrawls are deposited on the shells as the eggs descend through the oviduct just before laying. If the egg stalls, pigment becomes concentrated. If the egg twists, the pigment is laid on in scrawls. If the egg moves quickly, patterning is apt to be more sparse. Thus, upon returning to the cliff, one adult might claim a pale green egg with a lilac wreath at its wider end, while the bird next to it might settle on a dark brown egg with black scrawls, and a third might recover a nearly white egg. Experiments suggest, however, that the eggs' patterns function primarily as camouflage. In one study, white puffin eggs were repeatedly chosen by gulls over the murres' speckled eggs.

But what advantage can there be in such a dense population? Unlike terns and gulls, which collectively mobilize and fiercely attack intruders to their colonies, the murres are already in such an inaccessible location that viciousness toward humans and other mammals has not been selected for. Yet the sheer number of adult murres serves to protect the eggs and young from attack by avian predators, which are a constant threat. Since offshore islands are in great demand as nesting grounds by many species of seabirds other than murres, the cliffs, from the tumbled boulders below to the grassy turf at the top, are usually layered with populations uniquely suited to take advantage of each niche. While the murre colony occupies much of the midsection of the cliff face, pairs of large and aggressive glaucous gulls watch from above, each claiming not only a good-sized area of cliff top but that portion of the murre colony immediately below. One false move among the murres, and the gulls swoop in to steal an egg or a chick. There is usually a second population of glaucous gulls beneath the murre colony. These gulls scavenge the rocks and beaches for whatever gravity delivers from the murre colony, usually fallen eggs and dead and dying chicks. Among the other birds that share offshore islands

The eggs of the common murre are remarkably varied in color and pattern. The birds nest in dense colonies, and differences in color and pattern may help the parents identify their eggs.

with murres, either on the Atlantic or Pacific coast, are guille-mots, fulmars, cormorants, kittiwakes, storm-petrels, jaegers, razorbills, and herring gulls.

Living in such close proximity to one another, murres tend to do things en masse. Since courting and mating occur at approximately the same time, the resulting eggs hatch nearly simultaneously. The pair shares incubation, which lasts from 28 to 34 days, depending on the warmth of the nest site. Hatching can take up to five days once the egg is pipped, giving the adults and chick a long period to imprint one another's voices before the baby bird is actually free of the shell. Adults have even been observed bringing fish to unhatched eggs and attempting to feed them. Adults will not feed any but their own offspring. The

chick swallows a fish whole; if the fish is too big to swallow, the chick may sit for a while with the tail still hanging out of its beak while its stomach digests the first part of the meal.

The chicks grow quickly, lose their down at 20 days old, and are soon ready to leave the nest. In true murre style, all the chicks in a colony do this at about the same time, usually in the dark hours around midnight to avoid detection by the ever-vigilant gulls. There is a snag, however; because the chicks' flight feathers have not yet grown in, they are not actually ready to fly. The chicks grow increasingly agitated as the hour of "fledging" draws near. They approach the cliff edge and back off again, calling desperately, *wee-loo . . . wee-loo*, as they contemplate the thousand-foot drop to the dark rocks and surf below. The noise becomes deafening as the adult males, who are most commonly on the nest after dark, give encouragement. Finally, one by one the chicks hurl themselves into space, bouncing and rolling down the cliff face to the water. The males remain with the chicks over the next weeks as they head south toward their winter range, first swimming and eventually flying, once the chicks' wing feathers have grown in.

Meanwhile, the mothers of the chicks return to the cliffs to find their families gone. With fish in their beaks, they bow over and over to the empty ledges, and finally eat the food themselves. They remain on the rocks for a few more weeks, defending their territories, until they, too, head south.

Northern Fulmar

A very fat, fuzzy, dark gray chick sits on a grassy ledge of a small rocky island. Neither parent is nearby, and, in fact, it has been hours since anyone has appeared to feed or look after the chick. It waits alone, staring out to sea. A gull comes winging by at eye level to the chick, but instead of swooping in for an attack, it veers slightly off and keeps going. The chick follows it with its eyes, turning its head to watch it go, and then returns its gaze to the sea. Another gull comes by. It, too, does not even pause, but shuns the chubby little morsel on the rocks. A skua, known pirate species of the open ocean and a fierce relative of gulls, comes by the small island, but it wings on past, too. Why isn't the chick attacked and eaten? Where are its parents? And why is it so extraordinarily fat?

The chick is a northern fulmar. Fulmars are members of the shearwater family, pelagic birds that are rarely seen near shore unless sick or wounded. The first northern fulmar I ever saw up close was lying dead in the sandy parking lot of the beach near my home. With its strange, tube-shaped nostrils, typical of the shearwater family, the bird looked as otherworldly as the ocean it inhabits beyond the horizon. Other pieces of their natural history make fulmars remarkable: their longevity (it is estimated that they may breed until the age of 34); the fact that they don't breed until they are at least 6 and perhaps 10 or 12 years old; and the fact that incubation lasts almost 50 days (almost five times as long as some birds). In spring, the birds nest in small to large colonies. Each pair incubates a single, large, chalk white egg, out of which hatches one of these fuzzy gray chicks. The adults leave this chick alone for hours and even days at a time while they make flights often exceeding 200 miles from their islands for food.

NEST
On bare ground
HABITAT
Cliffs of offshore islands
EGGS
1, white
INCUBATION
50–60 days, by both parents
BREEDING RANGE
In the far north of both the Atlantic and Pacific coasts

The northern fulmar usually nests in large colonies, each pair incubating a single white egg in a shallow excavation lined with dried grass. Adults often fly hundreds of miles from the nest site, locating food by smell with their prominent, tubelike nostrils.

These long-distance flights are possible in part because, besides various fish and other sea life, fulmars eat a tiny crustacean called a copepod. Each copepod contains a tiny drop of reddish oil. This oil becomes up to 35 times more concentrated in the adults' bodies. Upon landing, the parent bird regurgitates this fatty concentrate for the chick, who eagerly sticks its whole head into its parent's beak. The chick is often fed over five ounces of this concentrate a day. Some the chick digests immediately, and some it stores for future nourishment — and for protection as well. If threatened, the chick can squirt the oil with astonishing accuracy two to three feet at its attacker. The oil breaks down the bird's waterproof barrier, exposing its inner down to the cold ocean water. Squirted on a gull, for instance, the oil could mean death. While the parents of the obese little terror make a habit of announcing their approach well in advance of arrival, should they accidentally get squirted, they are uniquely capable of cleaning their feathers and are not threatened.

Scanning the cliffs, one can see other similar fat chicks dotted here and there in the loose colony. Some are with their parents — handsome, thick-necked birds whose white heads and breasts stand out sharply against the blue-gray rock and the pink sea thrift that blooms on the cliff — but most are alone. On their nightmarishly rich diet, the chicks gain almost an ounce a day, mostly fat, until eventually they weigh twice as much as their parents. This fat tides them over during their parents' long absences and is replenished each time a parent returns. It is particularly important when, at roughly one and a half months of age, the chicks are abandoned for good. They fast alone on their rock ledges until their wing feathers grow in completely, transforming them into graceful, self-sufficient gliders. Not truly migratory, the fulmars simply move away from land for the winter, to skim and rest on the open ocean.

Killdeer

To observe a variety of birds and their nesting habits is to observe many different variations on spring. Imagine a strawberry field. The beds have wintered over and now the snow is melting, revealing the brown plants ready to sprout new leaves and begin flowering. Simultaneously, the killdeers have returned, welcome proof that spring is not just an idea but a reality verified by the birds. The birds search the soggy ground between snow patches looking for insects until warm days finally melt the snow and the strawberry plants begin flowering.

In preparation for picking, a worker numbers the rows, 1 through 74. The male killdeer makes test scrapes in the field, one in the path beside row 27, another in row 60, another in the short grass beyond the strawberry patch, waiting to see in which scrape the female will choose to lay her eggs. The middle of the path, about three quarters of the way down row 17, turns out to be just the right distance from the farmhouse and the access road to satisfy the female killdeer. She lays four eggs, speckled to blend perfectly with the surrounding gravel. In a manner typical of ground nesters that incubate several eggs with minimal nest material for insulation, she arranges the eggs with their pointed ends together so that she can completely cover them with her body. The sun is warm, and she waits. At her eye level, there are strawberry blossoms all around, white, five-petaled, each with a small yellow cone in the center. Bees travel past the killdeer on the nest, busy in their own world of nectar and pollen. The flowers are fertilized.

The male and female alternate warming the eggs, rolling them over with each return to the nest so that the yolk will not adhere to the inside of the shell. In the eggs, hearts begin beating. The flower petals drop off one by one, thin white ovals

NEST
On bare ground
HABITAT
River banks, lake shores, farmland, airports, mudflats. Also nests on gravel rooftops
EGGS
4, dark and speckled
INCUBATION
24–26 days, by both parents
BREEDING RANGE
Throughout most of the United States and Canada

falling onto the mulch beneath the plants. Within the eggs, the embryos gain eyes. The yellow cones of the strawberry blossoms lose their stamens and become fleshy and hard. Days go by, and they enlarge and turn pinky orange. Within the eggs, muscles develop on tiny limbs. The killdeers wait. A warm spell begins, and the fruit enlarges rapidly, the flesh turning red-orange, beginning at the top and spreading downward over each fruit until only the tips are white. It is time to start picking.

One morning, just as the light is good enough to distinguish red from green, the pickers arrive and are assigned rows. The male killdeer watches warily from the nest in the path by row 17. Far down at the end of the path, a picker squats down and begins his work. An hour passes, an hour and a half . . . there is no nest exchange this morning. The killdeer on the nest watches and waits. The picker works steadily, moving closer. As incubation progresses, many birds stick tighter to the nest than they might have earlier. The male killdeer does not move, though his muscles are rigid with energy. The picker rises and stretches, taking a break. It is too much for the killdeer. To save himself, he gives up the eggs. On tiny legs he vanishes unseen through the berries, then rises into the air and circles the field, calling loudly. His mate joins him, their calls adding beauty to the morning.

The killdeer is well known for its broken-wing display, which it uses to distract predators away from the nest. Other birds — several species of ducks, pheasants, some shorebirds, and even some songbirds — use similar ploys.

The picker settles back to picking, inching closer to the nest. The female now moves in. She drops onto her side and spreads her tail feathers, a flash of orange that makes the man notice her and her feigned broken wing. She cries loudly, drawing attention to her vulnerability. The picker looks up and watches. He calls to someone else to watch. But no one chases her. She dashes to the nest, covers the eggs momentarily and then leaves. The picker watches, then stands up and walks curiously and cautiously toward the nest. He sees nothing but gravel in the path. Even from 10 feet away the eggs are impossible to see. Ah, yes! There they are. The picker bends to gather white rocks in his hand, but when he turns back to the eggs, they have disappeared again. Suddenly they reappear two feet from his shoe. Carefully, without touching the eggs, he surrounds them with a ring of pale rocks.

In the morning the picker finds only bare gravel within the ring of white pebbles. The killdeers fly over the field, calling loudly. There is no sign of young. A raven, early in the morning? A raccoon? The picker does not know, but clearly putting white rocks around the otherwise invisible eggs was not a good idea.

Whip-poor-will

NEST
On leaf-covered ground
HABITAT
Deciduous and mixed coniferous
forests
EGGS
2, white with pale splotches
INCUBATION
19–20 days, by female only
BREEDING RANGE
Nests in the eastern half of North
America, the Southwest, and
occasionally in wooded areas of
Southern California

We are walking in a deciduous forest in North Carolina — or
Maine, or perhaps Wisconsin. It is an early morning in May, and
the spring air is cool. We dig our feet in sideways to make our
way down a steep hill slippery with maple, beech, and oak
leaves. It is almost easier to just slide than to try to break our
speed. Then, all at once, practically from under my boot, a bird
flies up with the grace and silence of a huge brown moth and
disappears into a stand of pines nearby. The woods are suddenly
made mythical by this creature. We have heard them in the
night, and then too, they were mythical, calling their own names
over and over, relentlessly: *whip-poor-will, whip-poor-will, whip-
poor-will* . . . on and on until a person has to choose to love the
sound or hate the bird. The repetition feels vital, like the insis-
tent exuberance of a healthy child. "I am the damp night woods;
love me," it seems to say.

I sit on the side of the hill, where I have dropped in surprise.
I look down and there, by my foot, startlingly white, are two eggs
where moments before none existed. The hen has let me nearly
step on her before taking flight. The leaves are flattened from the
weight of her body, beautiful brown oak leaves pressed to the
earth. It is startling how plainly visible the eggs are, their pale
gray speckles little help in blending them with their surroundings. Unlike the killdeer, whose eggs are camouflaged by their
coloration, it is the whip-poor-will's own body that provides the
disguise. The whip-poor-will makes no nest at all, perhaps because any disturbance of the forest floor would actually make
her conspicuous. Instead she rests on the leaves like a leaf herself. With rounded wings that break the air silently, only at the
last minute will she lift off and disappear. We move away quickly
so that the hen can return and continue incubation.

During the next full moon, the eggs will hatch. The female's reproductive cycle is closely timed with the lunar cycle. On most nights of the month, the nocturnal insects on which whip-poor-wills feed are on the wing yet still visible to the birds only during the twilight hours of dawn and dusk. When the chicks hatch and demand food, however, the whip-poor-wills fly through bright moonlight, their huge mouths gaping wide as they catch the moths they so resemble. The chicks are semiprecocial; that is, they are covered with down and able to walk, but they remain near the nest to be fed. Thus they are able to stay warm and hide from predators in the moonlight while their parents catch food for them.

Whip-poor-wills are monogamous. After these chicks are raised, the parents will likely return next year to this same bit of forest floor to lay new eggs, though no nest has been built. Thus they are drawn again and again to a place upon which they have virtually no impact, a fact that for me only adds to the whip-poor-wills' mothlike lightness.

Ducks

Green-winged Teal

NEST

On the ground; made of grass, sticks, and leaves, lined with dark brown down pulled from the hen's breast

HABITAT

In tall grass and shrubs on the shores of lakes and ponds

EGGS

6–18, creamy white

INCUBATION

By female only

BREEDING RANGE

Near bodies of water throughout nearly all of North America

Most of us take ducks for granted. They are part of American mythology. They appear on lots of greeting cards for "Dad," I guess because all dads are supposed to want to go out and hunt ducks on some level of their psyches. Like cumulus clouds or amber waves of grain or majestic mountains, endless flocks of ducks like those that rose off lakes as settlers moved west are part of our national identity.

Yet ducks have experienced a head-on collision with Mom and apple pie. Most of the wheat for the crust of that pie is produced in the prairie pothole region, a vast, pocked landscape formed by the retreat of glaciers 10,000 years ago. Rich glacial till covers much of the middle of North America, including parts of Wyoming, Montana, and Alberta on the west; Saskatchewan, Manitoba, the Dakotas, and Nebraska to the east; and most of Minnesota, Iowa, Wisconsin, and Michigan. Over the last 200 years, acre after acre of this fertile ground has been put into production, resulting in the loss of millions of depressions — ephemeral pools and permanent wetlands — that traditionally offered nesting habitat for ducks. The crux of the problem is that our own bread basket is also the single most important breeding area for North American ducks. Half of all of our ducks nest there. Yet it is now estimated that, largely because of agricultural pressures, fewer than 15 percent of their nests are producing successful hatches.

The rich smell of willows is welcoming; we have trudged more than a mile over disturbingly barren, flat ground and wheat stubble. There are other willow thickets, farther off in the distance, isolated by the immense barrenness, and there is probably water there, too. The farmer has been paid by the government to leave this bit of ground undrained, but his plow and combine have cut close to the pool, leaving only a thin margin of vegetation. Suddenly a mottled brown duck hen, a green-winged teal, rises straight up out of the thicket in front of us. Keeping our eyes on the spot she has left, we prolong our intrusion for just a moment to look at the nest. But even with the margin of vegetation around the pool so diminished, there is no indication of where it might be. Anxious to be gone and leave the hen in peace, we search the willows just a moment longer, parting some tall grass to suddenly reveal a delicate heap of the hen's own down. It is a startlingly private sight. We back away and leave. Beneath the down, however, had we pushed it aside, we would have seen 11 hastily concealed eggs.

Ducks, like other waterfowl, do not have brood patches, featherless areas that permit the eggs to come in direct contact with warm skin. Instead, the female pulls downy feathers from her own breast to line the nest and cover the eggs whenever she is absent. The male does not help with nest building nor with incubation of the eggs. After the hen lays the first egg, she loses interest in her mate, and he eventually goes off to join other males for the summer. This is not the result of "laziness" or any other character flaw, but simply another solution arrived at through the process of evolution. As is the case with other species, such as hummingbirds, in which the male is brightly colored, attractive plumage might alert predators to the whereabouts of the nest. The female duck, on the other hand, like the female hummingbird, is virtually invisible on the nest, and so is better off carrying on most of the reproduction of her kind alone, without any help from the male.

Though the hen lifted directly off the nest when we approached, after we back away, she returns through the underbrush on foot so as not to reveal the location of the eggs to potential predators. If we could peek through the willows, we

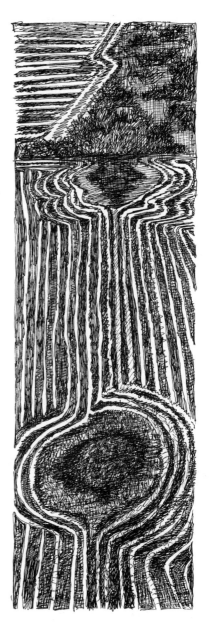

would see her move the down aside with her bill before she settles on the eggs, turning them and drawing in more of the surrounding vegetation. While ducks do not actually pick up material and fly or walk with it to the nest, as do more sophisticated nest builders, throughout egg laying and incubation the hen adds material to the nest by drawing it from the immediate surroundings with her beak.

Most ducks cope with the precariousness of ground nesting by reaching full breeding maturity in just one or two years and by laying lots of eggs in each clutch. A ruddy duck, for example, may weigh only one pound, but lay 14 eggs weighing a total of three pounds! A single duck hen can handle such large numbers of chicks only because they are precocial, that is, hatched with feathers and "ready to go," and because they hatch out simultaneously, as opposed to sequentially. The eggs hatch simultaneously because the hen waits to begin incubation until she senses that her clutch is complete. Once hatched, the young spend a few hours imprinting on their mother's appearance and then follow her to the water in an obedient little group.

But why do 85 percent of the duck nests on the prairies fail to produce young? Why, when most ducks are capable of living 15 to 20 years, do most survive only a few years? If we could watch this same little puddle of water and its surrounding willow and cattail thicket tonight, in the dark . . . if we could crouch here, invisible and with no smell to our bodies, we might very well see, off in the distance, approaching from the next thicket, a dark shape materialize into the form of a delicate fox going about the business of hunting to feed her young. She would very likely not miss our thicket. In such a stark landscape, it is obvious where the nests are going to be. She comes closer and, with her keen nose, it takes only moments to locate the nest. The hen may fly or may herself be captured. If she is killed, the fox will likely first cache the eggs for a later meal and then trot lightly off to her den with the duck hanging from her mouth. Dropping it off for her kits, she may not return for the eggs immediately but go on to see what other nests the night may yield before dawn.

But haven't there always been foxes? Surely ducks must be adapted to cope with them. To understand the problem, one must look back to the prairies as they existed before European settlers arrived. Then the marshy pothole region was vast. A predator searching for food had to negotiate a much more complex and irregular terrain of sloughs, ponds, and ephemeral pools, all of which were surrounded by vegetation that was much less starkly defined than that spared by man and his plows. Today, the modern landscape goes by formula. Thus, a fox need merely ring a pond, scanning a narrow swath with its nose, to quickly locate its prey. The ducks' problems are compounded by factors such as drought, which makes peninsulas out of islands, with deadly consequence.

Another significant change is that when the settlers arrived, there were wolves. The people found the wolves dangerous and frightening, so they killed them off, and coyotes gained dominance. The coyotes, in turn, became pests, so their numbers were reduced. Wolves and coyotes tend to eat mammals rather than birds and their eggs. They also tend to keep smaller predators, such as foxes, out of their territories. Thus, when wolf and coyote numbers fell, the stage was set for the fox to take over.

European settlers planted trees, and crows moved in, taking advantage of this new cover as they feasted on the rich diet the prairies had to offer, including an abundance of waterfowl eggs and young. Settlers erected buildings and created piles of rocks, wood, and debris, and raccoons moved in, benefiting from the newly provided shelter as they too tapped into the wealth of waterfowl nests. Uncontrolled hunting by humans at first did not make a dent in the vast waterfowl populations, nor did the acres of land drained for agriculture. But as the numbers of hunters continued to increase and agribusiness took over, new and insidious killers compounded the situation. Chemical fertilizers, herbicides, and pesticides began to concentrate in the water holes of the prairies; traditional menaces such as botulism, parasites, and disease increased their threat as waterfowl populations

became overcrowded in the reduced habitat spared by agriculture, development, and drought.

   As I have researched this book, I have developed some irritating habits, such as spontaneously waking up at three in the morning, unnerved about my children's futures. At these times, sleep is impossible, and I have learned to get up and get busy. I go downstairs and write, and then, when dawn is just beginning, I put on my shoes and go for a walk. I wish I weren't writing about ducks in late fall. The other morning as I walked briskly down Main Street, past neat houses newly decorated for Christmas, all at once I heard a volley of shots. Four miles away, in the wide delta of the Eel River, the half light was no doubt revealing ducks just leaving the delta for the ocean. The pastel delicacy of the dawn had left me off guard. I found myself standing alone on the sidewalk, in my quiet little town, suddenly swearing out loud.

Ducks have precocial young. This means that the ducklings are hatched with their eyes open, protected by down, and are able to walk and leave the nest within a day or two of hatching. By contrast, altricial hatchlings, such as those of a robin, are naked and helpless.

The names of ducks read like poetry to me — canvasback, pintail, old squaw, ruddy duck, green-winged teal, cinnamon teal, blue-winged teal, bufflehead, harlequin, goldeneye, eider duck. Given what ducks are up against and how few of them are left, it is unimaginable to me that someone would actually want to shoot one. I have killed lots of domestic animals for food, so many that I wonder about my lack of reaction when I lop a chicken's head off and gut it. But when I imagine a pintail out on the delta just lifting off the water and suddenly shot down, I mentally double up. To compound the matter, it is estimated that for every bird actually bagged, 1,400 pellets of shot are left behind. Many ducks, including pintails, redheads, canvasbacks, and mallards, inadvertently pick up these pellets as they feed, mistaking them for seeds. One swallowed shot is enough to kill a duck from lead poisoning. A hopeful note, however, is that despite the fact that unimaginable millions of lead pellets remain in our wetlands, lead shot is now illegal and is being replaced with steel shot. Perhaps, with the banning of lead shot, we are beginning to make the changes necessary to preserve our ducks before their diverse and lovely populations are beyond saving.

The ruddy duck (right) can produce three times its own weight in eggs in a clutch; the hen may weigh only a pound but lay three pounds of eggs.

Geese

A favorite metaphor of those trying to emphasize the importance of saving wetlands is the image of the driver who discovers, after a long day's journey, that the gas station, restaurant, and motel at which he was counting on stopping have all been closed down. He drives on into the darkness, unaware that there will not be another gas station for over a hundred miles. Or, to put it another way, could you drive from California to Alaska with only two or three gas stations or rest stops along the way? During incubation, a goose may lose up to 40 percent of her body weight. Thus it is imperative that she build up reserves on her way north so that she is in top condition to withstand the bitter weather of early spring and the rigorous demands of nesting. Yet we have decreased and eliminated critical stopping places along our four flyways with too little thought for the needs of the migrants.

Geese, however, are doing much better than their smaller relatives, the ducks, in large part because geese generally breed farther north than ducks, out of direct competition with man. In fact, while we often speak of ducks and geese in one breath, they actually are remarkably different in a great many ways. For instance, ducks do not mate for life, but form new pairs each fall or winter for the next season, the drake accompanying the hen to her hatching place. Geese, however, choose one partner for life. Generally only death will separate them and cause the remaining goose to choose a new mate. Male and female geese both return to their natal breeding grounds, nesting and later migrating in family groups. Thus, there is considerable inbreeding among geese, resulting in extended families that may include yearlings as well as middle-aged and older members, which may still be breeding at the age of 40. Among Canada geese, the ex-

Canada Goose

NEST
On the ground; a heap of grass, moss, and sticks lines with down from the hen's breast

HABITAT
Open tundra; shores of lakes, marshes, meadows, and islands

EGGS
4–10, white

INCUBATION
25–20 days; by the female, while the male stands guard nearby

BREEDING RANGE
From approximately the middle half of the United States northward

clusiveness of these extended families has resulted in 11 distinct races. These races vary from the tiny "cackler," which is not much larger than a mallard, to the "giant" Canada goose, which can weigh up to 24 pounds. The races have subtly different markings and vocalizations and, while they may inhabit the same breeding range, they mostly do not interbreed.

On a knoll that offers good visibility of the surrounding marshland, last year's grass is dry and flattened by snow. New grass pokes through, but it offers little cover for the goose who watches from a nest of reeds and cattails that she has scraped together with her beak and lined with soft gray down from her breast. Beneath her large body are five white eggs that she has incubated for nearly all of the 28 days necessary for hatching. With

While the male Canada goose does none of the incubation, he is extremely vigilant while his mate is on the nest and after the young are hatched.

so much time invested in incubation, instinct causes her to stick ever tighter to her job.

When a fox appears in the distance, trotting, sniffing, the range of possible reactions for the goose and gander is much wider than for a solitary duck hen. Unlike ducks, most of which have legs set quite far back on their bodies, making them awkward or nearly helpless on land, the legs of geese are positioned in the middle of their bodies, making geese agile walkers as they graze on grass and defend their nests. Now, the goose flattens herself on the nest, laying her neck out straight on the ground and waiting motionless, while the gander runs at the fox with neck outstretched, hissing his warning. The fox immediately gives up any idea of attack. Knowing the power of a gander's strong wings and fierce bill, he trots on.

The goslings all hatch within 24 hours of one another and are soon ready to leave the nest, one parent in the lead and the other parent guarding from behind. As the goslings grow, the adults molt their wing feathers, first one adult and then the other. This way, they are not both flightless at the same time and are better able to defend their young. Once the goslings have fledged, it is time to head south. I can't look at a flock of Canadas without wondering what it would feel like to fly with the wind sliding along my neck, geese before me, geese behind, geese distantly to my side, calling to stay in contact, heavy wingbeats audible through the clouds. Because family units migrate together, the geese flying with me would not be strangers, but my family, my mate, this year's young, my mother, my father, aunts, uncles, cousins for generations.

Canadas and other geese face more acute dangers in their wintering grounds than in their nesting areas. Geese winter on and near water all across the southern tier of the United States. In California, they head for the Central Valley. The refuges in the

Central Valley are strangely concentrated, Edenlike compounds where there are not only immense flocks of snow and Canada geese, but red-tailed hawks seemingly in every tree, great horned owls sitting almost in plain view, white pelicans feeding dance-like in the cattails, and ruddy ducks, pintails, gadwalls, and wigeons encountered in profusions in the pools. On the map, the refuges look fairly generous, large, green, squared-off shapes set aside for birds to simply rest and rebuild their strength. Any-one who has not actually visited one of these refuges might think we are taking adequate care of our wildlife. But often half to two thirds of each refuge is open to hunting, and the wa-terfowl jam themselves into the remaining free zones. During a recent trip to one of these refuges, my kids sat on the top of our van, mittens and wool hats on, staring upward, soaking up the sight of thousands and thousands of geese, while armed men with dogs waited in the ditches behind the levees for a duck or goose to miscalculate an arrival or departure and fly within range. It was an odd atmosphere, disturbing one mo-ment and supremely magnificent the next, as wide V after V crossed the sky.

California Condor

A hot, dry wind rises from the rugged canyons below and whistles up through the long flight feathers of the female condor's wings. It is her mate's turn to brood the egg in the cave. Her view of the mountains widens as she rises on a thermal of hot air, yet she scrutinizes each canyon minutely. She is an immense bird, twice the size of a turkey vulture. A relic of the Pleistocene Epoch, over a million years ago, she is here alone, with her mate and their one chalk white egg, which the male now holds on top of his feet beneath his glossy black body. Her eyes pass over the tumbled boulders lodged in the narrow ravine where their cave is hidden. Onto the bare dirt floor, one week before, she laid the large white egg from her customary standing position. The egg hit the ground but did not break.

Her eyes are keen. In the next valley she spots a shape that was not there yesterday. She knows the valleys' contours by heart. She tips a wing and angles over to look more closely. A coyote, dead. There is not a lot of hurry in a condor's life. The dead do not run. She and her mate will wait until the flesh has softened with time and decay, and she drifts off to check other carcasses. Her head is pinky orange, bare skin that will clean easily after she has poked it between the coyote's ribs. Her size distinguishes her from a vulture, as does a large white triangular patch beneath her wing that has caused many human hearts to suddenly race. A condor! It is a rare sight that was once common. From British Columbia to Baja, condors were plentiful when European explorers first arrived. Whales, seals, deer, elk, bighorn sheep, and pronghorn on which the condors fed were plentiful as well. But in their last holdout, south of California's San Joaquin Valley, they have fed on dead range cattle and poi-

NEST
On bare ground of caves or inaccessible cliff ledges

HABITAT
Once nested from British Columbia to Baja

EGGS
1, white

INCUBATION
42–50 days, by both parents

BREEDING RANGE
Extinct in the wild, but being reintroduced in the Sespe Condor Sanctuary, Los Padres National Forest, in Southern California

soned bait intended for coyotes, and on the poisoned coyotes themselves.

By 1940, only about 60 condors were left. In 1946, there was concern enough over the condor's fate that a sanctuary was set aside in the rugged dry mountains north of Los Angeles. Eighty-three square miles of dry terrain became the Sespe Condor Sanctuary. Yet condors left the sanctuary, ranging 50 to 80 miles away to feed, and people hunted the huge birds for sport. Condors consumed lead fragments from bullets in carcasses and died from lead poisoning. Egg collectors stole the condors' huge eggs. DDT gained popularity as a pesticide, and the condors got their dose at the top of the food chain. In 1954, condors came under the protection of California state law, yet their numbers continued to decline. In 1967, the U.S. government stepped in and listed the condor as one of the first federally recognized endangered species. Numbers continued to drop. By 1981, there were 21 condors left in the wild. In 1983, there were 19; in 1984, there were 15, with only five breeding pairs. Since a condor chick requires more than a year of parental care to reach maturity, these pairs could only have been expected to breed every other year, if they had survived. By 1985, there were only nine individuals left in the wild, and only one breeding pair. That year, the female of that last remaining pair died from lead poisoning. In 1986, there were three condors left in the wild, all of them males. In 1987, the last remaining wild condor, a bird with the unpoetic name of AC-9, was captured.

Even as condors were vanishing from the wild, however, a captive breeding program began at the San Diego Wild Animal Park, and the numbers began to reverse themselves. In 1988, the first captive-bred chick was hatched. In 1989, four chicks hatched; in 1990, eight more were hatched. That same year, Andean condors were released in the area of the Sespe sanctuary

Condors, like their relatives the vultures, lay a single egg on bare ground. Each egg weighs over ½ pound and is laid from a standing position.

and given plenty of lead-free carcasses for food. In 1991, 13 California condor chicks were hatched, bringing the total of California condors in captivity to 52. In the fall of 1991, two of these captive-bred birds were finally released back into the wild.

Naturalist Ken Brower once said, "When the vultures watching your civilization begin dropping dead . . . it is time to pause and wonder." Perhaps we are beginning to do more than wonder. Perhaps someday a pair of condors will again share the incubation of an egg until, one day in April or May, the egg tooth of a chick protrudes from the shell. Perhaps the huge birds will gently nibble away the shell that holds their chick and regurgitate into its gullet a warm carrion soup that is not laced with lead or cyanide. Perhaps someday we will again be able to watch condors in their courtship flight, wingtips nearly touching in air as they spiral in circles above the canyon.

It takes a pair of condors a total of about 18 months to produce a single chick able to fend for itself. Five months of care are required before it can even walk away from the nest site, still unable to fly.

Marbled Murrelet

Before 1974 I would not have given a second thought to placing the marbled murrelet here with the ground nesters — if I included it at all. Before 1974 it was one of the least known birds in North America. Only four nests had ever been found. These were all in Alaska, most typically in the bare gravel of wind-blown mountainsides, but one, surprisingly, in the branches of a low tree. What confounded biologists was that the discoveries of these few Alaskan nests could not account for the relatively large populations of murrelets in British Columbia, Washington, Oregon, and California, not only in winter but during the breeding season. Scientific literature does not usually bear titles such as "Enigma of the Pacific" (Guiguet, 1956) or "The Mystery Deepens" (Jewett, 1934), but biologists simply could not explain where each year's crop of juvenile marbled murrelets was being hatched.

What little information was known only seemed to confuse matters. Adults were observed flying far inland, carrying fish in their bills. Unattended downy nestlings were found on forest floors, seemingly dropped from heaven. The staunchly non-metaphysical speculated that, since the birds need to be elevated in order to achieve adequate lift when they leave the nest, the birds must have been hatched in the crevices of inland rocky cliffs. But no nests were found. Cash rewards were offered to anyone who could solve the mystery by such respected sources as Arthur Cleveland Bent, the author of a series of birding bibles, Life Histories of North American Birds, and by the Audubon Society, but only scattered clues came in.

In fact, the marbled murrelet has the distinction of being the last native North American bird to have the location of its nest discovered. In 1953, loggers in British Columbia cut down a

NEST
No nest built; egg is laid on moss on wide limbs of old-growth trees, also on bare ground among boulders

HABITAT
Nests in old-growth forest; also on windswept mountainsides in Alaska

EGGS
1, greenish with pale speckles

INCUBATION
27–30 days, by both parents

BREEDING RANGE
Pacific Coast from Alaska to Northern California

large hemlock and found among the debris a marbled murrelet with a brood patch. Pieces of eggshell were also discovered. A Canadian ornithologist who had been searching for the nest of the marbled murrelet for 20 years wrote that the logger "was very close to the nesting Marbled Murrelet that day." But no nest was found. Unknown to North American biologists, the mystery was solved with the discovery of a nest in Siberia in the 1960s, but this information was unavailable in the West. The answer was right under everyone's nose — or, to be more specific, far above it.

Through a lush, old-growth rain forest in coastal California, a footpath makes a cool and winding cut through a delicate carpet of ferns and oxalis. Overhead, far above the world of humans, the canopy of this great forest is a private place, veiled in lichens, inhabited by flying squirrels and red tree voles. The early twilight of dawn is filtered wetly through fog, and throughout the canopy there is constant dripping, as the needles comb the moisture from the air, gathering the tiny cloud droplets into larger drops that fall down through the trees, eventually watering the plants' roots.

This forest is predominantly made up of redwoods and Douglas-fir. Compared to the thousand-year-old redwoods, the huge, lichen-covered Douglas-fir trees are young, having lived a mere 500 to 600 years. Yet their limbs are bigger in girth than the trunks of most trees. A certain broad limb of a giant old topless fir is covered with thick moss and centuries-old lichens and littered with a duff of fallen twigs and dead needles. Only a slight turn of its head reveals the murrelet's presence on the branch. Though the bird and the one glass-green egg it incubates are hundreds of feet in the air, there is no nest. Only a depression in the bed of thick lichens made by the weight of the small bird's

body contains the egg. A second bird appears, penetrating the open canopy like a bullet, stalling for a split second above the massive branch, then dropping and walking up to take its turn. A redwood forest is a strikingly silent place. The murrelets' soft notes of communication are audible for some distance. Seconds later, the bird that has been on the nest leaves, flying directly toward a creek that runs nearby and following it downstream and out of sight.

This was the world that a tree surgeon entered on August 7, 1974, when, 137 feet up in a tree, he accidentally knocked a

For years, marbled murrelets were observed flying inland over the forests of the Pacific Northwest. Though ground nests had been discovered in Alaska, it remained a mystery where more southern populations were being hatched.

strange, mottled chick to the ground. When the nest was finally found, it was nothing more than a depression in the moss of the giant branch, ringed with droppings. Subsequently, other nests were located, all of them in old-growth trees, causing scientists to suspect that the murrelet may be dependent on the continued existence of old-growth forest for its survival in the lower 48 states. One nest has been found to which the adults had added twigs, but most of the nests in old growth have had no material added. Rings of droppings found around some nests are probably not deliberately deposited by the adults to contain the eggs but rather accumulate once the nestling has spent some time in the nest. Thus the branch on which the murrelet's nest is built must be wide enough to keep the egg and nestling from falling off. Horizontal branches in nest trees such as the Douglas-fir are not likely to grow into massive platforms until the trees are nearly 200 years of age. Moss and lichen seem to play a role in keeping the egg and chick on the branch by offering a malleable substrate. Lichens do not form a deep mat until they have been growing on a branch for at least a hundred years.

The discovery of these first nests stepped up the urgency with which biologists have pursued information on this previously little-known bird. Different definitions of the term old growth produce only slightly differing estimates of how much is left. The old-growth forest that once stretched 2,000 miles from Alaska to Northern California is nearly gone. Of the redwoods, which were the dominant tree of this forest in southern Oregon and Northern California, less than 4 percent remain. For those who see in a downed giant not a nurse tree that would be home to thousands of species as it decomposes but potential board feet, allowing a tree to fall and rot is a moral crime that robs food from the mouths of children. When a sawmill closes, whole

A marbled murrelet nestling is brooded by its parents for only a few days. After that, the chick remains alone on its branch, day and night, hundreds of feet in the air. Its parents return from the ocean only at dawn and dusk to bring their chick fish to eat.

towns are left without income. Generations of human relationships are suddenly shattered. Yet dwindling forest reserves and
automated mills are realities that won't go away. To those people
whose livelihoods do not depend on cutting down those last
fragments, there seems little question that these inspiring last
stands should be spared.

After the murrelet egg hatches, the nestling is brooded by a
parent for a day or two and then left to shuffle around on its
branch alone. Its parents resume their ocean life, returning
morning and night with fish, while the murrelet chick remains
arboreal for 28 days. For an alcid, this is a relatively short "childhood," resulting in fewer trips inland with fish for the parents.
As the nestling matures, its juvenile feathers grow in but remain
bound in their sheaths with the mottled down still attached at
the tips. Thus the nestling continues to blend with its surroundings. A day or two before it is to leave the tree, it is abandoned by
its parents. The baby bird preens off all of its down in the last 24
hours before it fledges and emerges as a sleek black and white
bird, now camouflaged for life on the ocean. But it is still hundreds of feet from the ground, perhaps 30 or 40 miles from
the sea.

How a marbled murrelet fledgling leaves its branch is still
a matter of speculation. Unlike many species of songbirds, in
which the young make test flights before leaving the nest,
the alcids, most notably the murres, generally simply plunge.
"Plunge" is not an understatement for the tiny murrelet. Like
many other seabirds, it has a large body relative to the size of its
wings. This makes diving into the ocean easy, but maneuvering
in the tops of redwoods is less than graceful. The sheer height
and open canopy of the old-growth tree may be essential for the
fledgling to freefall through the air until its tiny wings are moving fast enough to bear its weight. To imagine plunging half-

grown out of the top of one of the tallest living things on earth, and flying 20 or 30 miles to an ocean I have never seen, untethers my imagination. It is the stuff of which perhaps not headlines, but certainly myth, is made.

Unlike murre chicks, which are met by a parent when they enter the water and taught to fish as they are accompanied on their way south, once a murrelet chick reaches the ocean, it must learn to swim and catch fish all alone. Nonmigratory and normally relatively solitary, the murrelet will likely spend the winter near shore, simply diving for small fish and invertebrates by day and sleeping on the water at night.

4
Platform Nests

~

A platform nest is simply a loose heap of unwoven sticks and vegetation that a bird assembles as a place to lay its eggs. Bitterns and cormorants build platform nests on the ground. Grebes' nests, rather exceptionally, float on the water. But the most revolutionary development was the building of the elevated platform nest.

It is tempting to imagine a bird, stick in beak, flying to a tree and saying to herself, "If I can just get these sticks to stay in the crotch of this branch, I can lay my eggs up here, and we'll all be a lot safer." But, of course, natural selection does not work this way. There are no Thomas Edisons or Alexander Graham Bells in the bird world. No "Come here, Mr. Watson's." The evolution of the platform nest was no doubt unimaginably gradual. The flourishing of mammals favored getting eggs farther and farther up, off the beaten track. In the process, nesting took on fascinating new dimensions as birds adapted to all of the obstacles and possibilities afforded by the exploration of trees and shrubs for nest sites.

The great blue heron nests in colonies in the tops of trees. The nest is made of sticks that are not woven together but simply lodged in the forks of branches. A colony of these long-legged waders looks strangely precarious.

Egrets and Herons

Great Blue Heron

NEST

Platform of sticks lined with finer material, high in trees

HABITAT

Lakes, marshes, bays, estuaries; occasionally on cliffs

EGGS

3–6, blue-green

INCUBATION

28 days, by both parents

BREEDING RANGE

In appropriate habitat throughout most of the United States

Great Egret

NEST

Flimsy platform of sticks, unlined or lined with finer material

HABITAT

Lakes, marshes, bays, estuaries

EGGS

1–6 (usually 3), blue-green

INCUBATION

23–26 days, by both parents

BREEDING RANGE

Common in the southeastern United States; also in the far West and in the Atlantic states

An egret fledgling dangles upside down by one long leg, desperately flailing with the other for a second grasp. It rests a moment, its white wings pulled downward by gravity, and then begins flailing again. No one in the nest above seems to notice. No parent's face looks over the edge. No one squawks in panic. There is simply the din of everyday squabbling and grousing. The white form again struggles desperately and then simply gives up, exhausted, dropping 40 feet into the thick, green swamp water below. If this were a movie, there would have been dramatic music to build the suspense, and sad music when the young egret vanished out of sight. But in nature, death comes without music.

Looking up into an egret and heron rookery, it is hard to imagine that any security at all has been gained by elevating nests. Long-legged waders, the birds appear out of their element balancing on flimsy collections of sticks that are not woven but simply piled in the trees. Pale blue-green eggs are sometimes visible through the bottom of a nest. Occasionally a foot may poke through the wide mesh of sticks. The smell of excrement and regurgitated fish permeates the air, and the birds constantly grumble, as if the presence of hundreds of their own kind offers no comfort in numbers, but only irritation.

In the daily life of a colony of egrets and great blue herons, the toppling of a young bird out of the nest is not a tragic accident. The parents are quite attentive while incubating their eggs. They share nest duties, changing shifts with elaborate displays that allow time for the incubating bird to identify its mate before being approached. But once the eggs hatch, life becomes increasingly ruthless. The eggs hatch sequentially, because incuba-

tion begins as soon as the first egg is laid. Thus the three or four eggs in a normal clutch hatch over as many days, giving the older chicks considerable advantage over their siblings.

Both parents feed their young, catching and swallowing small fish and then returning to the nest to regurgitate partially digested pellets into the bottom of the nest. The chicks dive for these pellets, the strongest chicks getting the largest share. As the chicks mature, they begin to "scissor" their parents' beaks, demanding the food directly. Especially when food is in short supply, the older chicks often attack younger siblings and drive them out of the nest to their death, committing what is known by the grim name of "siblicide." Thus the herons have in place a sort of brutal insurance policy. In years when food is scarce, the oldest chicks have a decided advantage and are likely to survive. During years when there is an abundance of food, all of the chicks may reach maturity, building up a reserve population for the future.

Before the commencement of the breeding season, both the male and female egrets acquire long, flowing, white nuptial plumes. These plumes, however, were almost the egrets' undoing. Beginning in the mid-1800s, for over half a century it was the style to adorn hats with the long egret feathers. If feather gatherers could have simply picked up the plumes when the birds shed them at the end of the breeding season, it wouldn't have harmed the egrets. But by then the feathers were usually too worn to suit milliners, so the hunters killed the breeding birds during nesting. It was reported that at a single London auction almost 50,000 ounces of feathers were offered for sale. Four birds were killed for each ounce of feathers, and for each pair of adult birds killed, three or four eggs or young also died, so this one auction cost the lives of perhaps a million egrets. Compound this over a half century of auctions in North America and Europe, and it becomes clear how close the egrets came to disaster.

Fortunately, early environmentalists were horrified by this slaughter and began writing articles and proposing legislation to save the birds, resulting not only in the egrets' protection but in the formation of the first Audubon Society in 1896. Now, as I drive the freeway near my house, egrets are such a common sight that generally no one in the car even points them out. But I watch them and silently cheer. Imagine that my children look on these incredibly magnificent white birds stalking the sloughs 20 feet from our car as commonplace! I luxuriate in their indifference.

In 1903, the nuptial plumes of the great and snowy egrets were selling for $32 an ounce. Adult birds on the nest were slaughtered so that these plumes might be acquired in good condition.

Mourning Dove

NEST
Flimsy platform of twigs lined with finer materials

HABITAT
Suburban areas, farmlands, open forest, desert

EGGS
2, creamy to pure white

INCUBATION
13–14 days, by both parents

BREEDING RANGE
Throughout the United States except for high mountain regions

It is early morning in the Mojave desert, yet already there is a suggestion of the heat to come. The air has a sort of force, a momentum that makes it easy to imagine that in a few hours the temperature will be over 100 degrees. Yet now there is a breeze, and cumulus clouds ride overhead, moving east across the bluing sky.

We cannot look up for long. We have to watch our step, not just because of snakes but because all around us there are cactuses. The ocotillos do not pose a problem, nor do the saguaros. They are lovely, flowering at this time of year. It is the chollas that are a threat. Walking in a stretch of desert thick with chollas is an uncanny sort of experience. Actually, the cholla's whole common name is jumping cholla. When I was a child, my father told me to be careful of the cholla, and I always did my best to keep a deliberate distance. Yet on one of our expeditions, though I thought I had stayed at least two feet away from the cactuses at all times, suddenly there was a piercing pain in the back of my calf. I twisted around to look down, and, there on my pant leg was a spiny yellow-green cactus joint. I remember feeling convinced that cactus came after me. And the thing about chollas is that they don't just pierce and let go. They are wickedly barbed, so that removing the spines is almost impossible. How do you even hold onto the prickly segment in order to try to start pulling? That day, I learned to respect the jumping cholla in one quick lesson.

Yet as we walk, carefully, keeping guard, our eyes are lifted by a cooing sound. Mourning doves. What a welcome, soft sound. We look around, but there are no trees nearby. We look on the ground, but the doves are not on the sand. We wait for each call, using it to try to zero in on the birds' whereabouts. I raise my binoculars and am startled to see a dove in the middle of a clump of cholla! She is on a nest, a soft brown bird with a delicate beak and black eyes. She is not particularly afraid, and it is easy to see why. No one, not snake or fox or coyote or man, would dare go near this nest. She looks admirably complacent in her well-chosen surroundings.

There is cooing again, from the distance, and again the female on the nest answers. A second dove flies to the cholla, a male, bringing a delicate twig to add to the nest. He lands carefully and passes the twig to the female, who arranges it in the platform she is building. Doves make oddly minimal nests, whether they are nesting in a pine tree or an apple orchard or a cholla. I have seen dove nests so flimsy that I wanted to add twigs myself, to keep the eggs from falling through the bottom. This nest in the cholla is made of mesquite twigs, gathered, most likely, from the trees along a dry wash in the distance.

Beneath the dove, in the darkness of her soft feathers, there will soon be one and then two white, glossy, unmarked eggs. Each night, when the foxes and coyotes roam the darkness around her, the female will warm the eggs. And in the mornings, when darkness lingers in the long shadows of the giant saguaros, the male will take over, using his body first to warm the eggs and later to insulate and shield them from the midday sun. For two weeks, while the parents incubate the eggs, the surrounding cholla will keep them safe.

But what about a dove nesting five feet off the ground in a low pine tree in New Jersey? What keeps it safe? As with every species, if we look closely, we can see logic behind the mourning dove's survival. Camouflage is at work to some degree. The parent birds are a dull brown that blends with the shadowy branches and trunk of the tree. But there is a more important defense at work. Like their relatives the passenger pigeons, which were once so abundant in this country that passing flocks darkened the sky for hours at a time, the mourning dove is highly productive. Since its eggs require only two weeks of incubation to hatch, and the nestlings are ready to fly after only two more weeks, and the young leave their parents only one week later, each brood requires a total of just five weeks' care. In New Jersey, the dove may raise from two to five broods per nesting season. Farther south, in Florida, the same dove would probably nest year round, producing eight or nine broods a year. Out of perhaps 25 eggs laid per year, the loss of a few nestlings now and then would have little impact on the survival of the species.

In addition, doves and pigeons have a physical capability favoring their survival that is unique among North American birds. During the last few days of incubation, both the male and female produce a milklike substance in their crops. Production of this pigeon milk is triggered by the hormone prolactin, which is responsible for milk production in female mammals. Pigeon milk is extremely rich, containing 25 to 30 percent fat and 10 to 15 percent protein. Newly hatched domestic chickens fed on a mash containing the milk grew 16 percent heavier than chicks on normal feed. While the chicks of many seed-eating birds are carnivorous, being fed insects by their parents as a source of protein needed for growth, young members of the pigeon family are vegetarian, relying on the crop milk instead. In order to consume the curdy liquid, the newly hatched nestlings, blind and helpless, stick their beaks into the throats of the adults as the milk is regurgitated. An interesting and perhaps related characteristic of this family is that all members drink by sucking up water with their bills, much as a horse drinks, rather than tipping their heads back to let the water run down their throats, as other birds do.

After only three weeks of parental care, two spent in the nest

Pairs of mourning doves mate for life. While the male brings sticks during nest building, the female actually does the construction. Incubation is done by both the male and female, working in shifts.

and one after fledging, young mourning doves leave their parents. The mourning dove is classed as a game bird in many states, and mortality is high during the first year. It is, however, a beneficial consumer of waste grain and weed seeds. Some people look on them as pests, on a par with their cousins, the pigeons. But I have always loved mourning doves. They used to sing in the eucalyptus trees around my house, and as a child I often lay awake in my bed listening to their soothing music. Doves' refined appearance, paired with their remarkable adaptation for survival, make a comforting combination. Perhaps they are destined to hold their own with us long after other more delicate species are gone.

Bald Eagle

NEST
In top branches of a tall tree or on a cliff; made of large sticks, lined with grasses, moss, and twigs
HABITAT
Near lakes, rivers, ocean; nest usually has good visibility of surrounding area and often overlooks water
EGGS
1–3, bluish white
INCUBATION
34–36 days, by both parents
BREEDING RANGE
Much diminished in most of the United States; found in Pacific Northwest, Great Lakes, Atlantic and Gulf states

The giant old white pine towers above the forest. Its top is rarely even visible from the ground, and then only to one who knows it is there and is looking. But few humans venture to this remote country, where there is not even a fishermen's trail along the river. For those who frequent the air above the treetops, however, the forest giant is a landmark for miles around. And, conversely, its top offers visibility of the entire valley.

For 23 years this tree has been occupied by bald eagles. Twigs and branches, some of them six feet long, have been carried in talons and lodged in a fork near the top of the tree. Year after year, pair after pair, branch after branch, 23 years of building have resulted in a wood pile that rises eight feet up the trunk of the tree. Now, on top of this immense heap stand two adult eagles. We have seen them so often as symbols that their prominent white heads appear to have been put on their bodies simply to contrast artistically with the background of a flag or crest. In a tree, or flying, they still look like symbols, photographs, cut out and pasted on the landscape. To see eagles going about their own business, not for display but as real birds, is at the same time slightly surprising and deeply thrilling.

The nest is more than six feet across. In the middle is a hollow lined with moss and pine needles into which the eagles are staring. Three white eggs lie starkly visible on the moss. Their nest is so high and remote, and their parents are so fierce, that the eggs have no need for camouflage. The eagles watch intently because the first of the eggs is starting to hatch. The chick's beak protrudes from the shell. Although the chick must work hard to penetrate the thick shell, it is lucky that the egg was strong enough to bear the adult eagles' weight during more than a month of incubation. An eggshell weakened by pesticides would have been no match for an 8- to 9-pound male or a 10- to 14-pound female. But in this remote country the eggshell is strong.

The eaglet finally hatches, and its fine gray down dries rapidly. Four days later, the second eaglet hatches. One parent is always in attendance, watching the growing family. Three days later, the last chick hatches. An afternoon breeze blows through the valley. Far below, the river is a green and white ribbon, white where it tumbles off boulders and a still, brownish green in the pools. If the fishing is good for the parents, all three eaglets will survive. If the fishing is not good, by the end of nine weeks, when the eaglets might all have been ready to leave the nest, there may well be one lone eaglet sitting on top of the eight-foot-high pile, receiving all of both parents' food and attention. The others will have been victims of siblicide, payment on the insurance policy that has helped promote survival of the species.

With acid rain taking its toll, particularly in the eastern half of the country, traditionally good fishing lakes and rivers are losing their fish populations. This is a problem that extends the reach of man's effects into the remotest backcountry of the northern United States and Canada. Out in the West there are other problems. When I walk along our local rivers, I often see silt covering the rocky bottoms. This silt is washed down from clear-cuts upstream. Salmon, which a very few years ago were plentiful, are becoming scarce in this area. They cannot spawn in silt. When you look down in one of our streams at spawning time and do not see a single fish, the questions begin arising all too fast. What about fish eaters like the eagles? What about the ospreys? What about the kingfishers and the mergansers and the cormorants that all call a river home?

Yet, thanks to the banning of DDT, the eagles are coming back. A friend of mine once told me that having children makes one an optimist. Before I had children I doubted her. Now I understand. When you have children, you have to visualize a nation fit to live in, the kind of place over which only 400 pairs of eagles may have flown in the early '60s, but where 2,660 pairs flew in 1989 and perhaps four or five thousand pairs will fly by the year 2000.

Harris's Hawk

NEST
Platform of sticks, roots, and
other woody vegetation, lined
with grass and leaves

HABITAT
Deserts, particularly with
saguaros, mesquite, paloverde,
ironwood, cottonwood; also
riparian forest

EGGS
3–4, white

INCUBATION
33–36 days, by both parents

BREEDING RANGE
Southern Arizona, New Mexico,
and Texas; Mexico

In a large nest built in the crotch of a tall saguaro, a dark chocolate-colored hawk is standing, holding her wings out from her body, casting shade on three light brown, down-covered nestlings. She stands quietly for about 10 minutes and then abruptly begins to chirp, watching overhead as a male hawk appears with a mouse. He passes over the nest and lands in a paloverde tree next to another hawk, which by its similar size appears to be a male. He gives the mouse to this second hawk, who in turn flies to the nest and lands. The young chicks begin begging plaintively but with none of the usual aggression that characterizes sibling raptors at mealtime. The male offers the meat to the female, who proceeds to tear it into bite-sized pieces and calmly feed it to her young.

Thanks to spring rains, the cactuses wear jaunty orange, yellow, and fuchsia flowers, giving the scene a surreal quality. Why aren't these hawks fierce, lone hunters? Why are two males attending one female on the nest? Why is there no possessiveness either of mate or of food? Why are the chicks so passive toward one another?

Researchers who have been studying the Harris's hawk in the harsh environment of the Sonoran Desert in Arizona are beginning to come up with some convincing explanations for these hawks' seemingly laid-back attitude toward life. If we came back to this same place in the fall, timing our visit to arrive at dawn, we might well come upon a scene that would illustrate their findings. Imagine six hawks, silhouetted in the increasing light, sitting on a nearby power line. Below them, a black-tailed jackrabbit sticks its head out, intending to make one last foray before daylight. The hawks are instantly alert. In

an attack that seems planned, several hawks flush the rabbit into the open while another hawk swoops down from the side and seizes it with the talons of both feet. An adult jackrabbit is three times as big as an adult male Harris's hawk and two times as big as a female. The other hawks join in to subdue the rabbit, and then all settle down together to peacefully share their meal.

Biologists have determined that an adult jackrabbit neatly feeds five or six Harris's hawks at one sitting, which happens to be the average number of these birds that commonly winter together. In the desert, only small prey are available in the heat of the day, but for half an hour on either side of both sunrise and sunset, important windows on the night offer the hawks a brief chance at larger, more nocturnal prey. In order to take advantage of this short period, perhaps it has proved advantageous, if not essential, for Harris's hawks to be highly cooperative hunters. This cooperation may have carried over into the breeding season, when it is further advantageous to have an extra hunter providing food to the young, an extra sentry on alert, and an extra parent, should one die. Having helpers takes pressure off the primary nesting pair, often allowing for the rearing of a second brood each year.

Because of their cooperative natures, remarkable scenes are commonplace in the lives of Harris's hawks. It is not uncommon to see a hawk approach a solitary saguaro, then drop down and land right on the back of another hawk. The two hawks will often stand double-decker for a minute, until the lower hawk finally abandons its perch to the newcomer. This may be simply nonviolent perch-stealing, or perhaps it is the result of remarkably low personal space requirements. Observers have even spotted injured Harris's hawks being fed repeatedly and kept alive by others of their kind.

The variety of responses that birds exhibit in their family relationships is astonishing. Everyone agrees that birds are beautiful, but we do not usually look for much depth in their behavior. It is delightful to discover that cooperative behavior is much more common in birds than we might suspect.

Great Horned Owl

Snow falls and sticks to the hemlocks, weighing down dark green branches with steadily building loads. A male great horned owl flies silently through the dusky snowstorm, disappearing into the shadows between burdened branches to alight in a tall oak. Within is a large, snow-covered nest made of sticks. His mate does not budge from the nest but turns her head slowly 180 degrees at his approach. The smooth, slow movement does not disturb the inch of snow that has settled on her head. Over her back and the nest, the snow adds further insulation to the bark-colored feathers that protect her warm, downy body, which in turn protects the four large, nearly perfectly round, white eggs that lie snug in buff-colored down beneath her.

The male moves close and preens his mate's snowy head as she rises and simultaneously preens his snowless head, a gesture reflecting their cooperation in the shared task of reproduction. The eggs are exposed to the icy night air for only seconds while the female turns the nest over to her mate. On silent wings she leaves the nest tree, settling on her accustomed perch nearby not only to watch the forest but to listen. Almost no living thing is safe. Her year-round menu includes shrews, voles, weasels, squirrels, rabbits, house cats, skunks, porcupines, herons, pheasants, Canada geese, swans, hawks, barn owls, and screech-owls, as well as crickets, beetles, and grasshoppers.

But on this cold February night there are no crickets or beetles, nor swans nor pheasants. The owl swivels her head to listen when a mouse squeaks faintly from a tunnel beneath the snow. The dish shapes around her eyes help to funnel the sound to the asymmetrical ear openings on the sides of her head. This asymmetry helps her to pinpoint the source of the sound. She watches intently through the falling snow for any telltale evi-

NEST
Does not build a nest; takes over the nests of other large birds; also nests on protected ledges, in cavities and caves

HABITAT
Forests, swamps, orchards, deserts

EGGS
2–3, white, round

INCUBATION
26–35 days, by both parents

BREEDING RANGE
In appropriate habitat throughout most of North America

dence of the mouse's whereabouts. Muffled thumps are all that
can be heard as evergreen branches bend and finally drop their
loads of snow. Suddenly, a snowshoe hare bounds into the small
clearing, hastening toward the safety of the dark hemlocks beyond. The owl instantly readjusts her sights and launches into a
silent dive, at the last moment thrusting her head back and her
talons forward to sink them into the hare's back. There is half a
scream, then the white hare mysteriously ascends through the
falling snow, locked in the talons of its invisible captor.

On the owl's customary feeding perch, she pulls the hare into pieces and swallows it. Internally the fur and bones are separated from the meat and formed into a pellet that will be regurgitated by the owl. Beneath the owl's perch, beneath the layer of snow that now falls, strata of these pellets, feathers, bits of fur, provide a record of the owl's kills. After eating her fill, the owl returns to the nest with food for her mate and once again takes her turn at incubation.

Beyond the territory of this pair, which includes a little more than a square mile of forest and three small meadows, there are other nesting pairs of great horned owls. In each nest there are large numbers of eggs; four in one nest, three in another, and in a third, five. It promises to be an easy spring for the owls. Populations of snowshoe hares are up after a period of lean years when each nest contained only one or two eggs. Now, with the increase in the hare population, the number of owls will increase as well. Over cycles of about 10 years, this land seems to breathe in and out a scarcity and abundance of hares and owls.

A thaw melts most of the snow in the woods. Here and there hepaticas push through the deep forest duff and face their heart-shaped leaves and lavender flowers upward into the increasing light of a new year. After almost a month of incubation, the sound of faint peeping can be heard in the nest. The owl stirs and checks the eggs. Two have hatched, and two eggs remain hard and round beneath her. The nestlings peep again, but weakly. The chicks are unable to lift their heads or open their eyes. Unlike fully altricial chicks, which are born naked, the owlets are protected by an even covering of creamy white down.

While hatching for most seed-eating birds is timed to coincide with the ripening of their preferred seeds, the owls begin nesting while it is still winter, so they can hunt to feed their

Because great horned owls begin nesting in the middle of winter, their young are often ready to fledge by June. Juvenile owls leave the nest before they can actually fly and are fed and fiercely protected by their parents.

growing owlets before dense summer foliage reduces visibility. Members of the owl family do not build their own nests, occupying instead hollow trees, cliffs, caves, and the vacant nests of bald eagles, hawks, herons, crows, and occasionally squirrels. By nesting while it is still winter, the owls have their pick of nest sites, usually without displacing a family of the species that built the nest.

The female owl on the nest cocks her head slightly and eyes the sky. Two birds soar high above the woods in a rising spiral. A distant scream descends. And another. The red-tailed hawks are back. The owl looks up and follows the hawks, moving her head in the barest spirals. Last year, this was their nest. But they will not dare to contest the owls' occupancy. On the great horned owls' long list of prey are red-tailed hawks.

At three weeks of age, the owlets are half grown. The rim of the nest is littered with the remains of their partially eaten meals, the hindquarters of two hares, the tail of a skunk, and a sprinkling of duck feathers. The smell of decomposing meat and the scent of skunk hang in the air. In two weeks, when the young owls leave the nest, both parents will continue to feed them and guard them against predators, though few animals are likely to attack the fierce juvenile owls. At nine to ten weeks of age the young owls will fly, but they remain dependent on their parents for food while they learn to hunt for themselves. Once on their own, they will likely remain within 10 to 20 miles of the tree in which they hatched.

Pied-billed Grebe

NEST
Floating platform of rotting vege-
tation anchored to surrounding
plants
HABITAT
Ponds, marshes, lakes with reeds
and other vegetation
EGGS
5–7 bluish white eggs that become
stained brown during incubation
INCUBATION
23 days, by both parents
BREEDING RANGE
Throughout most of the United
States and Canada

Among the reeds near the middle of a marsh, a pied-billed grebe sits motionless on its nest, a small, brownish bird blending perfectly with the rotting remains of last year's vegetation. The marsh is small, but even a small marsh, with its channels divided one from another by tall rushes and cattails, offers ample privacy for secretive water birds like rails and soras and grebes. A black ring disrupts the form of the grebe's pale gray bill, like a permanent shadow cast by a reed. The bird turns its head alertly at the first suspicion of danger, and the "shadow" stays put on the bill. At the second suggestion of danger, the bird doesn't take a chance. As it rises, its eight eggs, once pale bluish but now stained a rich brown after nearly three weeks of incubation, are exposed for only a second. The grebe uses its bill to deftly push the damp lining of the nest up over the eggs and then slides soundlessly into the water. Diving would cause ripples. Instead, the grebe forces air from its feathers and body cavities and slowly sinks so that only its head remains above the water. Like a tiny submarine, it disappears among the cattails.

The pied-billed grebe, like its near relatives the loons, is above all at home in the water. Like a loon, its feet are placed well back on its body, making diving easy but land travel difficult. While loons usually nest on solid ground close to the shoreline, subjecting their eggs to the danger of rising water levels and passing land predators, the grebe's platform nest is actually a floating raft. Built of soggy, rotten vegetation and anchored to plants below the surface of the water, the interior of the nest may be actually wet. Within this damp hollow, the seven brown eggs remain utterly invisible beneath their cover of vegetation, while the grebe waits silently in the reeds for signs of danger to pass.

As inconspicuously as the nest was vacated, the grebe is suddenly back on the eggs. Approaching silently underwater, another grebe appears nearby. While the pair has shared incubation over the last several weeks, now, with the eggs about to hatch, the female incubates her clutch alone. The chicks that emerge from these shells will be among the most highly patterned of all newly hatched birds, clownish little nestlings with striped down. They are precocial and will be able to swim soon after hatching, but, like loon chicks, they will often choose to clamber up on their parents' backs to ride, resting and warming themselves in the sun. By autumn, however, ice will begin to encroach on the surface of the lake, and the juvenile grebes will get ready for their long migration, as far south as Central America.

5

Burrow Nests

~

I t is a little startling to imagine birds occupying underground tunnels and chambers, often nesting in complete darkness. Yet if we think in evolutionary terms, it is not hard to imagine a ground nester seeking the shelter of first one boulder, or perhaps two boulders together, or, even better, three, forming a safe crevice into which the bird can withdraw. In this shadowy shelter, the soil might be soft and easily scraped. The impulse to claw or dig with the bill either during courtship or, more likely, when a predator is sniffing around the area of the nest, might result in improved survival for the adults and young. Over millions of years, the tunnels deepened and digging became a way of life. Meanwhile, other opportunistic species employed the expedient alternative of simply moving into abandoned burrows excavated by other burrow-nesters.

The belted kingfisher nests in a burrow that is reached by a tunnel, up to 15 feet long, excavated into the side of a sand bank. Once hatched, the nestlings spend nearly three weeks in the total darkness of the burrow, being fed on fish by their parents.

NEST

A burrow, 3–15 feet deep, dug in a
bank by both male and female;
nest cavity is layered with fish
scales and bones

HABITAT

Vertical banks near fresh or salt
water

EGGS

5–7 (usually 6), white

INCUBATION

23–24 days, by both parents

BREEDING RANGE

Throughout most of the United
States and Canada

Belted Kingfisher

Cows graze on a high bluff overlooking the tops of alders that
line a stream below. They munch the grass, one cow trimming
the very edge of the cliff, oblivious to the dropoff beside her.
She is also unaware that beneath her back left foot, just below
the layer of topsoil, there is a hollow, spherical cavity, nearly 12
inches across and seven inches high. Within, it is totally dark.
There is the odor of fish and a dank, warm smell of soil and excrement. The floor of the cavity is rough with a wall-to-wall litter of clean white fish bones and scales. Six naked nestlings
crouch on this litter, keeping each other warm and waiting, listening to the sounds of the cow above until it finally moves.
Abruptly, one of the nestlings ejects feces onto the wall of the
cavity, then scratches at the dirt wall with its beak, bringing
down loose soil into the fish bones.

An adult male kingfisher's rattling call precedes him as he
rounds the bend of the stream beneath the top of the bluff, cutting through the alders. He calls again when he sees the cows and
lands on a dead limb in the treetops. He eyes the cows, then
darts into a small hole, about three inches in diameter and a foot
and a half below the top of the bluff, and disappears. The kingfisher makes his way up a slight incline, darkness gathering
around him as he moves four feet into the tunnel in the cliff. The
feet of the kingfisher and his mate are beginning to wear grooves
in the tunnel floor.

In the pitch darkness, the nestlings eagerly greet their parent, anticipating a meal of regurgitated fish. Both the male kingfisher and his mate have brood patches, and the male settles
down to warm the bare nestlings. Just five minutes later, however, another rattle call can be heard faintly through the tunnel.
The male immediately gets up, moves quickly down the tunnel,

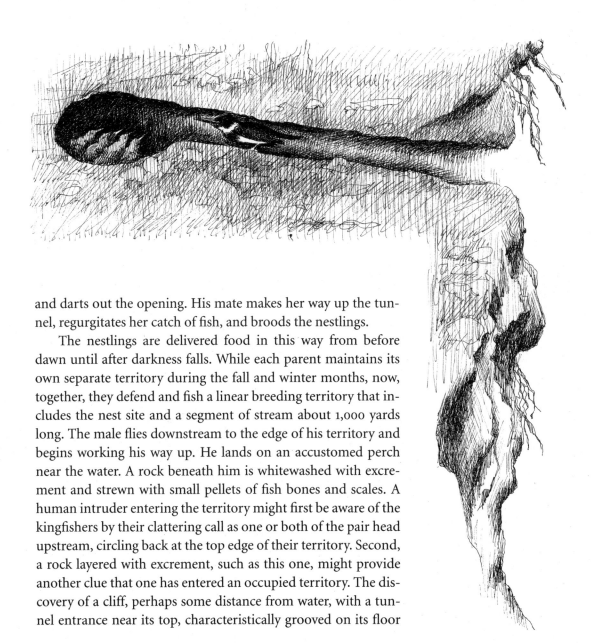

and darts out the opening. His mate makes her way up the tunnel, regurgitates her catch of fish, and broods the nestlings.

The nestlings are delivered food in this way from before dawn until after darkness falls. While each parent maintains its own separate territory during the fall and winter months, now, together, they defend and fish a linear breeding territory that includes the nest site and a segment of stream about 1,000 yards long. The male flies downstream to the edge of his territory and begins working his way up. He lands on an accustomed perch near the water. A rock beneath him is whitewashed with excrement and strewn with small pellets of fish bones and scales. A human intruder entering the territory might first be aware of the kingfishers by their clattering call as one or both of the pair head upstream, circling back at the top edge of their territory. Second, a rock layered with excrement, such as this one, might provide another clue that one has entered an occupied territory. The discovery of a cliff, perhaps some distance from water, with a tunnel entrance near its top, characteristically grooved on its floor

and free of spider webs at its mouth, would confirm the presence of a pair of kingfishers rearing a family.

From his perch the kingfisher tenses, stares into the water, and suddenly dives, fanning his tail feathers at the last moment to correct his aim. Just before disappearing under the water he shuts his eyes, and a second later he emerges with the fish in his beak. He returns to his perch, beats the fish to death on the limb, tosses it up in the air, and swallows it head first.

After the first week, the nestlings begin to grow feathers, but the feathers remain tightly contained in their sheaths for nearly two weeks. Thus the young, were they visible in the dark cavity, would look like odd little porcupines with dense coats of thick quills. On the 18th day after hatching, these feather sheaths begin

to split, and the nestlings abruptly become nearly fully feathered. Until this time the nestlings have had a special tip on their bills, presumably to protect them when scratching and pecking the cavity walls. This, too, is shed. A few days later, the nestlings make their way down the tunnel toward the bright sunlight at its entrance. As with most cavity-nesting birds, no time is spent fluttering around, learning how to fly. The nestlings poise at the mouth of a tunnel at the top of a 30-foot cliff, and their wings must work the first time they are tried. One by one, the nestlings become fledglings, crossing through the bright, sunny air that is alive with sound and motion, making for the alder tops nearby.

For the first few days, the fledglings stay near their parents, who feed the young birds as they get used to their new mobility. Then the parents begin to instruct them in how to catch fish for themselves, dropping dead food into the water for the fledglings to retrieve. Finally, about 10 days after the juvenile kingfishers leave the nest, they are able to fish independently and are driven by the parents from the breeding territory.

Burrowing Owl

NEST
Burrow of prairie dog or other mammal, often lined with dung and grass

HABITAT
Open grassland, prairie, and cleared areas such as golf courses and airports

EGGS
7–9, white

INCUBATION
21–28 days, by female

BREEDING RANGE
Appropriate habitat in scattered areas of the western half of the United States and Mexico; also southern Florida

A male burrowing owl busily goes about his business of the day, collecting dried cow dung in his beak and scurrying back to his burrow. He deposits it at the entrance, turns around and trots off to get more. Meanwhile, his mate carries the dung into the burrow and shreds it with her beak. No other owl so deliberately lines its nest. By the time this pair of burrowing owls stops its work, there is a ring of dung around the entrance to their burrow, and the tunnel and nest cavity are all lined an inch deep. This is clearly no casual endeavor. But what are the owls doing?

A likely answer comes a few nights later. A badger wakes as usual at dusk and sets off, hungry, to look for food. He is a powerful forager, keen-nosed and a fast digger. He takes a little detour up to some abandoned ground-squirrel burrows. He moves from hole to hole until he arrives at the burrow occupied by the female owl. She is heavy with eggs and has begun a two-week retreat, generally emerging only at dawn and dusk to receive food from the male until all the eggs are laid. Beneath her on the dung are the first two white, nearly round eggs. She has already begun incubation, so the chicks will hatch sequentially, rather than simultaneously. She hears the badger approach and stiffens. The sound of the badger's sniffing seems amplified, piped down the tunnel of the burrow. He pauses and rechecks the information that his nose has delivered. The burrowing owl is braced for the sound of digging to begin. In no time the badger could have his black nose shoved into the nest chamber, pausing to draw a deep breath of her scent before he collapses the burrow and devours the eggs — and perhaps the owl as well. But the badger smells only cow dung. He circles the hole to get another angle on the smell, and then, satisfied that the odor of dried dung has nothing to do with food, ambles on.

It has been observed that nesting success is considerably higher in dung-protected burrows. In Oregon, a study showed that of 25 nests lined with dung, only two were lost to badgers; while in the same location, 13 out of 24 unlined nests were lost. If the dung is removed from a burrow, it is usually quickly replaced by the owls. Interestingly, while cow, horse, and even dog feces are used, other material has also been found in burrows, including corn cobs, rags, gum wrappers, shredded newspaper, pieces of bone, animal remains, and a whole mitten. In one colony near a golf course the owls diligently went some distance to collect divots for their nests. Not surprisingly, nesting success was not improved with the addition of divots.

The burrowing owl is one of only two owls in North America that does not lay its eggs in an elevated nest. The other is the

The burrowing owl is the only North American owl to nest underground. It uses the abandoned burrows of mammals such as prairie dogs, badgers, and foxes, enlarging the burrow with its feet by kicking the dirt backwards up the tunnel and out the door. It often lines the entrance to its burrow with the dried dung of other animals, presumably to disguise its own scent.

snowy owl, which nests on the tundra. But snowy owls are commonly 24-inch birds with four- to five-foot wingspans. The male is a formidable defender of his nest, using outright attack and the more indirect "broken wing" ploy practiced by killdeers. The burrowing owl, on the other hand, is robin-sized, a mere nine or ten inches long. In this owl's treeless habitat, it is easy to see how hiding eggs in subterranean holes could easily evolve into the principal nest-defense strategy.

Traditionally, burrowing owls have been associated with prairie dogs, which like the owls live in colonies. It is hard to imagine a place that supplies more suitable nesting holes than a healthy prairie dog "town." The colony contains 30 to 50 burrow entrances per acre, each entrance leading to a tunnel that normally runs three to six feet beneath the surface for a distance of about 15 feet. Observers once thought the birds and the rodents

lived together, but actually the owls only nest in a burrow vacated by its former owner.

A prairie dog town established in a short- or mixed-grass prairie resembles a serene battlefield, with its mounds of dirt and burrows pocking the grassland. But the towns are actually rich and diverse islands of life in a wide, windswept sea of grass. In fact, one study identified over 140 animal and plant species associated with prairie dog towns. Bison and cattle are attracted to the many plants that thrive on the aerated, mineral-rich soil created by the prairie dogs' excavations. Insects and small rodents, finding travel easier on the town's bare dirt than in the surrounding prairie, are plentiful. They feed on the rich variety of leaves and leftover seeds and make use of abandoned burrows. For meadowlarks and grasshopper sparrows, the open ground is better for spotting seeds and insects. And, of course, attracted to all of this life are the predators — golden eagles, hawks, foxes, coyotes, bobcats, rattlesnakes, badgers, and owls.

Because both the prairie dog and and burrowing owl are relatively small animals living on wide and potentially dangerous open terrain, good visibility of the surrounding prairie is essential. Prairie dogs keep the grass trimmed, spending most of each day during the spring and summer foraging. Traditionally bison, and now cattle, help the prairie dogs keep the grass short around the town, giving both the owls and the prairie dogs a better view of predators from lookouts atop the mounds.

Burrowing owls and prairie dogs respond similarly to the approach of a predator. Alarm calls are sounded, the prairie dogs barking and the burrowing owls giving their *cak-cak-cak-cak* call. Depending on the location and type of predator, owls and prairie dogs may scatter, scrambling in crisscrossing beelines for burrows; or, if the danger is less imminent, the prairie dogs begin a chorus of barking, and the owls begin bowing and chattering. This bowing, strangely formal and controlled given the situation, may arise from a balance between the impulse to hide and the impulse to escape. Often the owl will bob up and down and rather comically turn its back on the predator as if attempting to make it simply disappear. This may be a move by which the owl readies itself to flee. Needless to say, a prairie dog town is a curious sight when all of this posturing and protest is underway.

Life in a prairie dog town is thrown into full gear by the melting of the snow in spring. In March and April the owls, which in the northern part of their range migrate south for the winter, return, both singly and in pairs. Each male of an already mated pair reclaims its burrow from the year before. Unmated males find vacant burrows and set to work cleaning them, kicking dirt backwards out the entrances with their feet. Courtship display takes place most commonly beginning an hour before dusk. In that delicate twilight, one can often just barely make out the owls. The prairie dogs have gone to sleep in their burrows. The heat of the day is subsiding. Over the western horizon, a clear blue-white sky is tinted with faint pastels, but the rest of the prairie is giving in to night. A high-pitched cooing begins, higher than that of a mourning dove. Then another. And from all sides, others. The darkened prairie is made wide again by the varying distances of the calls, some near, some far, just as the sky is made spacious by the gradual appearance of the stars. The male owls are singing.

At one burrow, a female is dimly visible sitting in the entrance near her mate. She suddenly gets up, and as she does the male stops singing. Like an uncomfortable adolescent, he stretches his wing and then his leg, then his wing again. The female joins in, showing that this is not simply some sort of shy shuffling but, like so much of courtship display, perhaps a display of "certificates of health," proof of soundness of wing and limb. The male begins singing again, this time stopping abruptly when the female makes a rasping sound. He suddenly flies off, but returns shortly with a kangaroo rat in his beak and approaches the female. She rasps even more insistently, and he sets it down near her. She continues rasping, and the male flies off again. This time he returns with a moth and gives that to his mate. The female is finally satisfied after the third trip. It is tempting to interpret this behavior as a ritualized test of capability to rear a family. She ceases rasping, and the two begin to nip gently at one another's bills.

The female then gets up, and the male stands tall in front of her, exposing two white patches of feathers that are not normally visible on his breast. His feathers are raised so he looks bigger than he really is. The female shows white patches on her breast as well, and the male mounts and copulates, singing as he does what is technically referred to by the poetic name of "song during copulation." The female responds with the "copulation warble" and the "smack" call, and the whole bout ends with the "tweeter." Afterward the male stands looking down at the female again, exposing his white patches, and then flies off.

Outside the burrows, which are occupied by the female owls, the diminutive males stand guard nearly 24 hours a day. By midsummer, the feathers of the little sentries will be sun-bleached lighter than the females'. Only the female develops a brood patch, and she alone incubates the clutch of eight white eggs, soiled brown from earth and flea excrement. The male seems never to sleep, leaving only to hunt or to take a break during midday, when the heat keeps the predators at bay. In the morning and early evening the female emerges from the burrow and gives the rasp call, sending the male off to forage for her food. For five or six weeks, the male feeds and guards the female and then the nestlings as well, until finally the family is too hungry for him to manage. It is about this time, approximately the first of July, that the young owls come out of the burrow for the first time, to stand near its entrance flapping their wings and hopping about, watching for a parent to return with food.

Unlike the young of most arboreal cavity nesters, who must be able to fly the first time they launch themselves without ever having had a chance to try their wings, the young burrowing owls have the luxury of flapping over the prairie, testing their landing ability on rocks or sticks, missing and falling. They also practice catching prey, taking turns pouncing on already dead insects. After about two evenings of actual airborne practice, the young owls are capable fliers, ready to forage with their parents. By mid-August their rasping calls for supplemental feeding are ignored by the adults.

Several people have fondly recalled to me their memories of crossing the plains by car or train and seeing prairie dog towns stretching for miles out the window, the little inhabitants standing on their hind legs to improve their visibility. Indeed, prairie dogs were once so abundant and widespread that naturalist Ernest Thompson Seton estimated there were 5 billion in the early 1900s. The largest prairie dog town recorded was in Texas. It measured 100 miles wide by 250 miles long and contained 400 million prairie dogs. This boggling amount of prime burrowing owl habitat makes me wonder just how many burrowing owls were there as well. Now the huge prairie dog towns have disappeared, their inhabitants poisoned by ranchers for decades. On a more hopeful note, burrowing owls have exhibited considerable ability to adapt to new environments, choosing marginal land such as airports and roadsides and areas disturbed by burning, grazing, and bulldozing, which offer wide visibility. In the absence of prairie dogs, the owl has adapted to using ground squirrel and other rodent burrows, provided there are perches the owls can use as lookouts.

6

Cavity Nests

~

Many species of birds nest in natural cavities for protection from predators and for warmth. Others have developed special adaptations that allow them to chisel out nest cavities where none previously existed. In the process of providing shelter for themselves, they also increase the number of cavities available to birds that are unable to excavate cavities of their own. Thus one species can become highly dependent on another species, and a decline in the numbers of an excavator species can mean hardship or disaster for others. The lives of cavity nesters are often good examples of just how entwined species in a given ecosystem may become.

The wood duck nests in natural cavities in trees or in nest boxes. The duck lays her eggs, one a day, into a lining of soft gray down that she begins to pull from her own breast after egg-laying begins.

Pileated Woodpecker

In Conrad Richter's book *The Trees,* there is a passage describing the wide expanse of virgin forest that once covered much of the eastern half of North America. This is the forest in which the pileated and ivory-billed woodpeckers lived for thousands, if not millions, of years, adapted to the primeval conditions. I still remember the upwelling of excitement that I felt as a girl when I first read Richter's book and began to grasp the vastness of the forest he was describing.

A family of settlers has just forded the Ohio River and come up over a rise to look out upon the land they are about to cross. "They had all stopped with a common notion and stood looking out," Richter wrote. "Sayward saw her mother's eyes search with the hope of finding some settlement or leastwise a settler's clearing. But over that vasty solitude no wisp of smoke arose. Though they waited here till night, the girl knew that no light of human habitation would appear except the solitary red spark of some Delaware or Shawnee campfire. . . . It was a picture Sayward was to carry to her grave, although she didn't know it then."

Richter describes their progress through that ocean of leaves: "Sayward watched her mother puttering along between the great shaggy butts that dripped with moss and moisture. All day she could see Jary's sunken eyes keep watching dully ahead for some sign that they might be coming out under a bit of sky. . . . You tramped day long and when you looked ahead, the woods were dark as an hour or a day ago."

This forest was cut down in the 18th and 19th centuries. By the early 1900s, both the ivory-billed and the pileated woodpeckers had nearly disappeared. As the forests regrew, however, the pileated was able to settle for second-growth trees, and in-

stead of going extinct it managed a gradual comeback. The ivory-billed, on the other hand, remained fatally dependent on a diet limited to the larvae of wood-boring beetles found beneath the bark of mature, dying, and dead trees. It is now thought to be extinct, though a remnant population may possibly survive in a remote area of Cuba.

When one begins to imagine the nesting season of the pileated woodpecker, one must first think *wood* — not planed lumber, but the rough bark of an old elm, scrutinized, listened to for beetles; the rotten core of a seemingly thriving beech, crawling with carpenter ants; the hollow branch of an old cottonwood, just right for the drumming tattoo of courtship; a punky old pine snag, prime for the excavation of a nest cavity.

It is a cool spring morning. On a bluff some distance from the Mississippi River, a pileated woodpecker appears and lands on the side of a tall pine snag, his feet planted two toes back and two forward, his claws gripping the smooth, bonelike surface. The bird is a male, his red "moustache" distinguishing him from the female. He does some exploratory tapping. He knows this snag well. He and his mate have occupied this territory for years. There are few other trees around big enough and rotten enough to excavate for nest cavities. The old snag is covered with holes of all sizes, carved not only by the pileateds but by the smaller woodpeckers in search of larvae and ants. There is a fresh cavity, which the pair began excavating and then abandoned, finding the heartwood there too hard to penetrate. Now the male circles the tree, testing the density of the wood. After some preliminary chiseling, his rhythm suddenly changes to a quick, stiff-necked drumming. The male has found soft wood in a location that seems right for a nest. Recognizing the rhythmic and tonal difference between excavation and communication, the female flies

over and together they test the trunk, tapping. The female taps to signal her agreement with the male's choice, and he begins serious excavation.

The pileated woodpecker is like a living carpenter's tool, a sleek composite of adaptations for woodworking. It has a strong, chisellike bill and powerful neck muscles for hammering. In order to withstand the constant beating, the woodpecker's brain is enclosed in a tough outer membrane surrounded by a space that cushions it from contact with the thick skull. Strong muscles in the head further absorb shock. The woodpecker's long tongue, with which it extracts insects from the holes it chisels, curls around the interior of the woodpecker's head like a tape measure in its case. The tip of the tongue is equipped with bristles that hold sticky saliva for extracting insects. Stiff feathers at the entrances of its nostrils filter sawdust from the air the woodpecker breathes. The woodpecker's feet readily dig into even a barkless trunk, while its tail serves as a prop. The rigid shafts of the tail feathers are bare at the tips, giving a better hold on the tree trunk. The central two tail feathers are so important, in fact, that they are not shed in a molt until their replacements have grown in.

Within a couple of weeks, the woodpeckers complete the nest hole and begin incubation. The dim interior still smells of fresh sawdust, newly excavated from the rotting heartwood and left in the bottom of the cavity as a scant layer of bedding. The male can feel the hardness of the four white eggs beneath him. The clutch is complete. For a little over two weeks, he and his mate will take turns on the nest. While the female will continue to occupy a separate hole in another tree at night, the male will spend each night on the nest. In addition, he will do the major part of the incubation during the day, spending a total of about

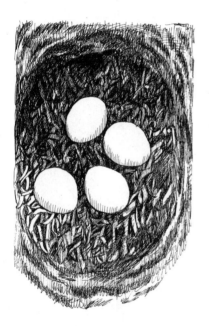

Members of the woodpecker family lay noticeably round, white eggs. Since the eggs are incubated in a cavity, there is no need for camouflage. Because there is nowhere for them to roll, they can be round.

18 hours out of each 24 on the nest, compared to the female's average of 6.

Inside the cavity, the air is still, cut off from the breeze outside that carries the territorial songs of neighboring warblers. A fly enters through a small hole above the woodpecker's head, explores briefly, then leaves through the sunny entrance. An hour passes, and then another, interrupted only by another fly and the steady visitation of mosquitoes tracking sources of blood. Abruptly the male hears wingbeats and the *cuk* of his mate. He stirs and taps on the raw wood of the inside wall. He pokes his head out into the bright afternoon. His mate is there to take her turn on the nest. They converse in low grunts. He looks both ways and launches from the rim of the cavity. She hops inside, briefly looks out of the mouth of the cavity to make sure the area is clear of squirrels or snakes or other dangers to her brood, and then settles down on the eggs.

Pileateds are very attentive parents, generally not leaving the eggs uncovered for more than a moment during nest exchange. Evidence of the birds' dedication was observed by a surprised naturalist and photographer, F.K. Truslow, in April of 1966. Sitting in his blind, Truslow had just photographed one nest exchange and was settling down for perhaps a two-hour wait for the next, when suddenly there was a crash, and he looked out to see that the whole top of the nest tree he had been observing for days had broken completely off just above the nest cavity! When the tree top broke off, the female, who was on the nest at the time, flew off to a nearby tree. Five minutes later she flew back to the nest, assessed the catastrophe, flew down to the fallen top where it lay on the ground, then worked her way back up the trunk of the snag. Finally, she disappeared into the then roofless nest cavity and, much to the astonishment of

Egg-carrying has been observed in several bird species, including the clapper rail, oystercatcher, mallard, shoveler, and merlin. The behavior in pileated woodpeckers has been documented in photos.

Truslow, who sat with his camera aimed at the jagged top, reappeared with an egg in her bill. He snapped his shutter madly as the female methodically came and went, carrying off all three of her eggs.

When the male returned about an hour and 45 minutes later to take his turn on the nest, he became instantly frenzied upon seeing the broken-off snag. After searching the area of the nest, he began calling frantically. The female reappeared, then flew off in the direction she had taken the eggs, while the male returned to the snag, as if in disbelief, to search the area again. When Truslow examined the old nest, he discovered that the woodpeckers had so completely hollowed the tree that the walls of the cavity were less than an inch thick. He never found the new nest, but he had succeeded in capturing rare documentation of egg-carrying in birds.

Of course, most pileateds rear their young much less eventfully. After two weeks of incubation, the eggs hatch, and the adults take turns warming their nestlings, the male doing approximately three quarters of the brooding. Both parents regurgitate ants, caterpillars, and other insects into the throats of their nestlings. The young birds eagerly suck and jerk on the adults' long, pointed bills. Life follows a rhythmic pattern of feeding and nest cleaning until, by the time they are ready to fly, the fledglings look like miniatures of their parents, their rakish appearance seeming a little precocious for young birds. When it comes time to leave the nest, there is no awkward and undignified crawling through the leaves, clinging desperately to branches. Instead, the fledglings spring from the cavity, looking every bit as trim as their parents. The family group generally remains together until autumn. Though pileateds do not migrate, the young may move as much as 20 miles from the territory of their parents.

The pileated woodpecker declined as North American forests were felled, but it has since shown a remarkable ability to adapt to life in second-growth forest, and its numbers have begun to increase.

Wood Duck

On the smooth surface of an old pine snag there are five holes made by pileated woodpeckers. The cavity second from the top, approximately 50 feet off the ground, is occupied. Within its dim interior, however, is not a woodpecker but a duck, who seems to float in a pool of her own soft gray down. She is a mottled color, with huge, glassy, black eyes ringed sharply with white. From within the pale down comes muffled peeping. Her clutch of 12 creamy white eggs is about to hatch. She kuks softly, teaching her young to follow even before they are free of the shell. Over the next two days the peeping gains volume and her replies become more emphatic until tiny beaks begin to break holes through the shells. Each duckling within its egg can hear the sounds of scratching and peeping from the other eggs, and soon the fluffy gray down of the nest is matted flat by the first explorations of 12 drying ducklings.

The next morning dawns clear. There is dew on the new green leaves of the surrounding treetops. The hen appears at the entrance of the cavity, looks around, and then abruptly flies off in the direction of the river, as she does every morning. About an hour later she returns. She flies very fast toward the hole and seemingly without slowing down disappears inside. Soon she reappears and perches on the rim, half in the cavity and half out. The dew has dried. The ground has warmed. She watches. She disappears into the hole but reappears in a few minutes. She perches again, motionless, watching. She tilts her head sideways. A crow wings over, surveying the morning, and the duck disappears into her hole. Ten minutes later she is back again, listening and watching. For no apparent reason she disappears again. Fifteen minutes later she reappears and watches, motionless. Min-

NEST
In abandoned tree cavities; lined with wood chips and down
HABITAT
Marshes, swamps, ponds, flooded forest
EGGS
6–15, creamy white
INCUBATION
28–37 days, by female
BREEDING RANGE
Eastern half of the United States; Pacific states; Wyoming, Montana; Mexico

utes pass. Finally, softly, she kuks. The coast has been deemed clear. Inside the cavity the kukking stimulates the ducklings. The hen makes a short flight to a nearby branch and then drops, spread wings breaking her fall, to the small clearing 50 feet below. From such a distance she looks very small, mottled like the leaves. She looks up and calls with increased energy.

Inside the cavity, the sudden departure of the hen causes the fluffy ducklings to begin throwing themselves at the bright entrance of the nest nearly two feet overhead. Finally, one duckling hooks the claws on the tips of its webbed feet into the wall,

scrambles to the rim, and looks out. A bright, wide world of treetops opens up. Other birds, at home in the leaves, sing invisibly at eye level, but the duckling's attention is focused on the hen's frantic calls coming from far below. Peeping anxiously, the duckling balances momentarily, spreads its insignificant wings and jumps into midair, outstretching its tiny, black, webbed feet as if to use every means available to break its fall. A blur of raw, bleached tree trunk and broken limbs, equal in height to a five-story building, flies past the duckling until the little bird suddenly collides with the ground and bounces into tall weeds between two fallen limbs. Instantly it springs up and dashes out of the grass to its mother's side.

One by one, the rest of the ducklings make the same jump. When no one else peeps from the nest, the hen sets out across country, her line of tiny triathletes behind, sprinting and hurdling over twigs and branches. The river is almost a mile away. This is quite an event for day-old youngsters of any kind, and the vitality of the tiny ducklings, as they roll and climb and tumble and race over the forest floor, through wild grape and Virginia creeper, seems all the more remarkable when one remembers that they have not yet had anything to eat or drink. The hen comes abruptly to a halt in the cover of thick vegetation that descends a sandstone bluff. She has arrived here every year almost to the day since she first made the trip as a duckling with her own mother. She pauses, watches and listens, then leads her ducklings down the bluff through the tangle until they drop to the barren gravel roadbed of a train track. She pauses again, listens, waits for two ducklings to contend with a large limb, then sets out across the tracks. The gravel pushes up under her yellowish webbed feet as she hurdles the first silver rail, crosses on a tie, and hurdles the second. She stops and kuks. As if they have been crossing train tracks all their lives, the ducklings spill across the gravel, climb onto the ties, jump until they clear the metal rails, descend the roadbed, and roll into the cover of brush where their mother waits.

They enter a glade of cottonwoods, alders, and willows. The ground is suddenly wet under their webbed feet, announcing with coolness the river's proximity. Then the sky opens up and the river stretches out before them. The hen takes in the fact that the water is low, leaving three feet of sticky mud and raccoon tracks between the vegetation of shore and the water. This means that on this side of the river there will be no shoreline cover once the ducklings are in the water. The hen pauses and watches. Downstream a line of barges is making its way against the current. She waits and watches. The tow pilot's charts show that the river at this point is better than half a mile wide, with a current of two to three miles per hour. Slowly the barges pass. The hen listens, unmoving, and then, without further hesita-

tion, launches herself. Her ducklings, not yet 24 hours old, pile into the water behind her. The current picks them up instantly as they begin to fight their way across the river. Twenty minutes later and far downstream, they slip into the forgiving current of an eddy that effortlessly takes them from the grasp of the river and lets them drift gently into the drooping branches of an old willow. In the privacy of shadow, with water under her belly, the hen rests. Her ducklings, too, rest momentarily. Then, catching sight of caddisfly larvae clinging to the willow twigs, they are set in motion once more, pursuing their first meal.

Before evening, the little family will float downstream to a place where the river has broadened out over the land into a marsh filled with duckweed and dragonflies and water mites and snails, rich diet and safe haven for 12 ducklings. Some of the ducklings will themselves serve as food for larger animals, but others will survive, and the hens will eventually return to their natal territory to raise ducklings of their own.

Elf Owl

In a dark cavity within a giant saguaro, an owl no bigger than a sparrow stirs and checks her newly hatched nestlings. The nestlings, covered with fine, white down, are the size of your thumbnail. The whole family, the three nestlings and the female — even her mate, who is somewhere out in the desert night — would fit on the palm of your hand. These are elf owls, the smallest owls in the world.

She hears the subtle whir of her mate's wings. Other owls that feed on warm-blooded animals fly silently, but there is no need for silence in the pursuit of scorpions, insects, and spiders. She shifts to the top of her nest cavity, and her owl face, with its round, yellow eyes, fills the two-inch hole in the side of the cactus. Her mate hovers momentarily and passes her a scorpion. The female settles back down in the cavity, crushes the scorpion in her beak, and eats it. Her mate flies off to glean insects from the bloom of a century plant. These will be fed to the nestlings.

The cavity in which the tiny owls are raising their family has a story of its own. It was excavated over a year ago by a pair of gila woodpeckers. It is approximately three inches wide and 12 inches deep, with walls that are now scarred over and hard. Some day, when this saguaro has fallen and decayed, this cavity may lie like a petrified gourd among the dried ribs of the fleshless cactus. A "saguaro boot," the Indians of the southern Arizona desert call it. In days past, it would have been taken home and used to hold food.

If it were to die, the giant saguaro would yield more than one saguaro boot, for above the elf owls' cavity there are three more cavities. One is occupied by gila woodpeckers, who take turns incubating their three white eggs; one is empty; and in the

NEST
In abandoned woodpecker holes; unlined

HABITAT
Desert with saguaro cactus and other trees, riparian woodland

EGGS
2–3, white

INCUBATION
24 days, by the female

BREEDING RANGE
Southern Arizona; scarce in Texas, California, New Mexico; Mexico

other, a female ash-throated flycatcher is sitting on four brown-scrawled eggs. But the saguaro may easily stand for a hundred more years, its cavities home to countless elf owls, ferruginous owls, screech-owls, flycatchers, woodpeckers, and flickers, as well as snakes, lizards, rats, and mice.

For nearly a month, the elf owl pair raise their nestlings in the cool cavity, insulated from the desert heat by the thick, succulent flesh of the cactus. Upon fledging, the juveniles emerge looking like drab, miniature adults. Both adults continue to bring food to the young owls while they learn to catch insects for themselves.

As agriculture and development spread over the face of the desert, they bring with them the spoilers of the peaceful scene above. Starlings flourish in a wide radius around cultivated fields and bird feeders, boldly displacing even gila woodpeckers, whose impulse to excavate is strong in winter but wanes during the breeding season. Perhaps this is because the walls of the cavities must cure for weeks before the woodpeckers can move in. Displaced woodpeckers that cannot find an empty cavity may wait out the breeding season without producing any young.

As with most desert ecosystems, sparse rainfall makes the saguaro community slow growing and sensitive to disturbance. A saguaro does not flower for the first time until it is about 50 years old. It takes over 75 years for it to begin growing the "arms" that give it its distinctive shape. And while many animal species depend on the saguaros for food, shelter, and nest sites, the saguaros themselves depend on the animals they shelter. Bees, bats, and woodpeckers are among the chief pollinators of the saguaros. While gila woodpeckers and elf owls can be found nesting in trees such as the cottonwoods, mesquite, and sycamores, the saguaro community is their principal habitat. It is a

The gila woodpecker, along with the gilded flicker, plays an important role in the deserts of the Southwest. Not only are these birds pollinators of the saguaros, they make their homes there, in the process providing homes for many other desert species.

unique treasure of interdependent plants and animals, many of which are found nowhere else in the world. This, of course, is only part of the reason it is so important that we safeguard the well-being of the habitat. Ultimately, it is for the sake of the individual animals who live there — for the sake of the seemingly insignificant elf owl, which weighs less than 2 ounces when fully grown but is one of the enormously fascinating jewels of our continent — that we should give the saguaro community our vigilant protection.

Barn Owl

In the evening light, an old barn stands at one end of a once busy farmyard that is now filled with brambles. The remains of a house have been covered over by the thorny canes, but among them in the front yard, lilacs and irises still bloom on schedule. When the rancher who bought the land on which the barn stands passes by each evening in his pickup truck, he is nagged by the barn's appearance. He intends to tear it down. He tells himself that kids may get hurt exploring it, but what is really bothering him is that it looks bad to have the barn slowly decaying. A barn is only as good as its roof, and in better light the roof is beginning to show bare patches where the wooden shingles have either blown off or simply disintegrated. With a new roof, the barn could last another hundred years. But the rancher doesn't need the barn. He needs money and time. With each farm that he has acquired in order to make his equipment pay, his debt and the list of jobs that need doing have compounded. So the years go by, and the barn stands abandoned.

Yet just as the irises and lilacs have continued to bloom without a gardener, inside the barn, life has gone on without a farmer. In one corner of the second-floor hayloft, spilling out of an old double concrete sink lying on its side, is a ghoulish accumulation of disintegrating dark gray fur mixed liberally with bleached skulls, delicate lower jaws and, visible if one looks more closely, thousands of diminutive femurs. Presiding over their heritage are 11 white, heart-shaped faces swaying back and forth, strangely illuminated in the dim light. If children did come to play in the barn, they would run home with stories that the place is haunted. Hissing screams mix with rasping snores as a pure white shape appears on silent wings, a cross between an

NEST
Unlined cavity in barns, steeples, silos; tree cavities, cliff crevices; becomes littered with fur and bones

HABITAT
Farmland, grassland, forest edges; may nest in towns and cities

EGGS
3–11, white

INCUBATION
30–34 days, by female

BREEDING RANGE
Throughout most of the United States where nest sites and adequate food are available; uncommon in the East

Barns, steeples, and silos in which barn owls might nest are often boarded up, excluding the owls. With large natural cavities a rarity, it is essential that barn owls be accommodated by humans. Barn owls are valuable neighbors: a single owl feeding a family catches as many mice, gophers, rats, moles, shrews, and other rodents as 12 house cats.

angel and a ghost. The dead mouse in her beak, however, brings the barn owl down to the level of reality. Two of the nestlings are crushed into the deep litter of mouse fur and dust as the others clamber over each other to reach the parent. The biggest and oldest gets the mouse. The two youngest and smallest pull themselves up again and join in the fight, but the mouse disappears in one gulp. No sooner is the mouse delivered than the white ghost rises silently back out the hayloft window and is gone, gliding down over a wide meadow that has yet to be incorporated into the rancher's rotation.

In the damp new grass, a diminutive shrew can hardly hear itself walk. It crosses a small patch of bare ground, following a two-inch-deep ridge in the soil. But when it continues its search for insects through a clump of dry weeds, it makes the barest sound, not much. The head and body of the shrew are just over two inches long. Its feet have the minutest pads and toes. But sound is the enemy of the shrew and of the mice that also forage in the darkness. Abruptly, there is a scream from above. The shrew freezes in terror, then is instantly extracted from its small world, lifted high up over its accustomed landscape and winged toward the barn loft window. The owl utters a rasping screech, which sets the nestlings in the barn hissing and slurping and clambering once again for position. Hatched sequentially, there is a 10-day difference in age between the two oldest nestlings and their youngest siblings. The youngest are again jostled into the litter of fur and mouse skulls, the shrew is swallowed, and the owl is off again, passing her mate as he returns with a catch of his own.

The barn owl is considered by many people to be the most valuable and most widespread bird species on earth, inhabiting every continent and most large islands except New Zealand. In many countries it is treated with great respect, not only for its

beauty but because it prefers a diet that is at least 95 percent rodents. Like other owls, the barn owl has relatively mild stomach acid that does not dissolve the fur and bones of its prey. Instead, a few hours after each meal, the owl regurgitates neat oval pellets of fur and bones that provide a precise record of the owl's diet. Lists of the prey vary only slightly from location to location. One study of 703 pellets yielded 16 bats, 3 rats, 930 mice, 1,579 shrews, 1 mole, 19 English sparrows and 3 other birds. Another study found 200 pellets to contain 454 skulls including those of 225 meadow mice, 2 pine mice, 179 house mice, 20 rats, 6 jumping mice, 20 shrews, 1 star-nosed mole, and one vesper sparrow.

A typical mouse can breed at around six weeks of age and give birth six to eight times a year to litters of four to six young, so one mouse's annual reproductive potential would be enormous should she and her offspring be spared "untimely death" by the absence of predators. Interestingly, barn owls also have a rapid reproductive rate. While most raptors take several years to reach sexual maturity and then raise only a single brood of a few young per year, barn owls are capable of breeding at less than a year old and can respond to an abundance of prey with two large batches of nestlings per year. Each of these nestlings is estimated to eat its own weight in mice each night, which can add up to more than 100 rodents per fledgling raised, or 1,000 per large brood per year. In one experiment, a nestling was offered as many mice as it could eat. It consumed eight mice in quick succession and just three hours later was ready for four more. It has been computed that to supply its hungry brood, each adult owl catches as much prey as 12 house cats.

Before the arrival of large numbers of European settlers, barn owls nested in natural cavities in cliffs and trees. While forest-dwelling birds such as the pileated woodpecker were thrown into decline by the relatively abrupt conversion of virgin North

Barn owl boxes can be secured where they will be not be disturbed: high on the inside walls of barns, on the outer walls of tall houses, or 15 to 20 feet off the ground on trees at the edges of fields and meadows. The box can be made of plywood and should be 16 inches on each side, with a 6-inch entrance hole, drain holes on the bottom, and ventilation holes on the sides. It should open for cleaning in the fall.

America into farm country, the barn owl benefited and flourished from the white settlers' appearance on the landscape. Grassland expanded, offering a rich population of rodents; buildings were constructed, providing abundant cavities for nesting; and rodents got a further boost in and around the buildings from a rich, relatively steady diet of stored grain. Since the 1930s, however, barn owls have been declining in number. Not only has foraging habitat been greatly reduced, but nesting sites have become hard to find. Old barns and sheds have been torn down, granaries made owl-tight, and churches with steeples replaced by more modern buildings. Open wells have become a thing of the past and hollow trees a rarity. In the Netherlands, farmers continue to construct special little doors that allow barn owls free access to barns and outbuildings. With this simple practice, or the construction and installation of nest boxes, combined with more moderate agricultural practices such as the protection of hedgerows, annual fallowing of fields, and restraint in the use of rat poisons, barn owls in North America might continue to delight us with their midnight screams outside our bedroom windows.

In the farmer's abandoned barn, the adult owls come and go all night, delivering their catches of mice. As the weeks go by, the four youngest owls get weaker and eventually starve. But the rest grow strong, their eerie hisses becoming increasingly louder and more demanding. Prey gets larger and feeding trips fewer. The largest owlets gulp down whole cottontails head first, the hindquarters stalled in their open beaks while the forequarters are digested. The nest area grows rank with the smell of ammonia and rotting, uneaten prey. The owlets practice flying and killing half-dead mice.

Finally, nine weeks after the first egg was laid, all of the surviving owlets have fledged but one. The parents perch high up on the loft window, each with a mouse in its beak, beckoning the young owl into the air. It flaps its wings and lifts off, teetering momentarily on the sill of the loft window to snatch a mouse and then launching itself silently over the meadow toward a stand of trees where its siblings have taken up residence. At the sight of an approaching owl, the young give loud, rasping hisses, begging to be fed. Just as the young owl swoops from the window with its parents following behind, the farmer passes by in his pickup, headed home after dark. He sees the three white owls and thinks about his barn. He says to himself, quietly, that the barn has been good for something. And he thinks that maybe he will let it stand.

Nuthatches

Red-breasted Nuthatch
NEST
In excavated cavity lined with
shreds of bark, roots, moss,
feathers, grass; occasionally in
abandoned woodpecker holes
HABITAT
Coniferous and mixed forests
EGGS
4–7, white, spotted with reddish
brown
INCUBATION
12 days, by the female
BREEDING RANGE
Northern United States, western
mountain regions; Canada

Ten feet up the white trunk of an old paper birch snag, a small hole about an inch in diameter is ringed by sticky amber-colored pitch. But anyone who has ever cut up birch knows that the trunks weep a clear, watery sap. And the days are long past when the wood of this old snag flowed with any sap at all. The glistening amber pitch does not even smell like birch — it has the pungent smell of balsam fir. A few inches above the round hole, a circle of perforations, like the work of a methodical child poking with a scissor point, has scarred over into a ring of black dots. The scene's curiously deliberate look is not relieved when a small bird comes hurrying, head first, down the trunk.

Perhaps it is the fact that they move upside down that makes nuthatches seem simultaneously so clownlike yet so capable. Not everyone can virtually defy gravity. That they sound like they are tooting on little tin horns — *wa wa wa wa wa* — leaves an observer convinced, deep down, that the little birds are there primarily for our entertainment, jesters of the forest. But, as with all nature, there is logic, however obscure, to each move. The nuthatches benefit by moving down trunks because they encounter insects that "upwardly mobile" woodpeckers and creepers have missed. The circle of dots on the bark can be explained by the fact that nuthatches lack adaptations for excavation such as the woodpecker's strong beak and neck. To penetrate tough bark such as that of the paper birch, it is easier for them to perforate and lift out a disk of the papery covering and then begin excavating the core.

But why do nuthatches smear pitch around their cavities? The origins of this practice are slightly more obscure. In North America there are four species of nuthatches; in Europe and Asia, an additional 16. Nearly all of these species occupy themselves in unusual and sometimes seemingly useless efforts at "home improvement." In the case of the red-breasted nuthatch, it may be that smearing pitch at the entrance of the nest cavity is an evolutionary relic that no longer serves a functional purpose. But red-breasteds do nest over a wide range; perhaps pitch-smearing repels insects, mice, or even reptiles in certain environments. Whatever the reason, the instinct to smear pitch is so strong that nuthatches nesting in deciduous trees, such as the paper birch, will fly to evergreens and carry pitch back in their beaks. Yet the pitch surrounding the nest entrance is actually a liability. The female, who does most of the egg-sitting, particularly at the beginning and end of incubation, often becomes increasingly disheveled from contact with the resin as she passes through the mouth of the cavity. Biologist Lawrence Kilham once found a dead female nuthatch stuck to the pitch of her own cavity, fortunately before she had had a chance to hatch young. To avoid this danger, the incubating bird usually flies directly into the cavity like a bullet, screeching to a halt before it reaches the back wall, or hovers momentarily before entering.

The red-breasted is one of the few nuthatches that excavates its own cavity. Most nuthatches use existing holes but busy themselves caulking cracks and crevices with fur, reducing the entrance size with mud, or, in the case of the white-breasted, smearing dead insects around the entrance. Both male and female white-breasted nuthatches tuck food into crevices of the nest cavity for later meals.

While feeding, the red-breasted nuthatch uses a crevice in the bark as a vise to hold food while it breaks off pieces small enough to swallow. The brown-headed nuthatch of the southeastern United States actually uses bark as a tool, holding a bark chip in its beak to pry under other pieces in search of food. Nuthatches in general are omnivorous; that is, they consume both plant and animal food. The red-breasted easily pries open evergreen cones for their seeds and eats beetles, caterpillars, insect eggs, wasps, flies, and moths as it forages out among the smallest twigs. During incubation and early brooding, the female stays on the nest while the male brings food to her. Mate-feeding is a significant part of courtship, perhaps as a sort of preview of the male's food-acquiring abilities.

Unlike woodpeckers, which are more classic cavity nesters — excavating their own holes, adding no material to the nest, laying pure white, round eggs that hatch into altricial young — the nuthatches' nests seem to hint at a more complex evolutionary past. The red-breasted gathers grass, rootlets, moss, bark shreds, and feathers to form a soft bed on the floor of its cavity. Here it lays four to seven white to slightly pinkish eggs speckled with brown. As with most songbirds, incubation does not commence until the last egg has been laid. Out of the eggs hatch chicks that are covered with dark gray down.

Once the nestlings have hatched, both the male and female work to bring them food. Not long after a nestling has eaten, it ejects a white sac from beneath its tail. Brisk as a maid collecting dirty laundry, one of the parents picks the sac up in its beak and flies off, dropping it to the ground on the way to look for more insects. Called a fecal sac, this neat packaging of fecal and urinary waste allows the nestlings to grow up in the confined cavity in relatively sanitary conditions. It is thought that the act of swallowing food stimulates the nestling's body to eject the sac. Since a parent is usually still present in the nest, this often makes for timely removal. In the first few days, these fecal sacs are often eaten by the adults, giving them much-needed energy; but as the nestlings grow, the sacs are transported away from the nest site and dropped. Maintaining a clean nest not only keeps down parasites and disease but cuts down on odor that might attract

keen-nosed predators. The nuthatch is not alone in using this neat system of sanitation. The formation of fecal sacs is characteristic of most "perching birds" and woodpeckers.

After more than two weeks in the nest cavity, the young nuthatches are ready to fledge. The repeated comings and goings of the parents have littered the entrance and passageway to the cavity with plant matter and dirt. The little birds, almost as large as their parents, make their way up the passage and cross the sap without sticking. One fledgling tries its wings, attempting to flap them in the narrow mouth of the cavity. Its sibling, now eager to reach the light, crowds from behind. One by one the nuthatches spill from the cavity, squeaking and peeping excitedly, some half hopping, half flying to a nearby branch, their long claws already gripping the bark. The father bird scurries headfirst down the white trunk toward his expansive brood, as if to demonstrate right off just how clever a nuthatch is expected to be, and soon the little fledglings are nearly as agile as he is, gleaning insects for themselves from the trees.

Eastern Bluebird

An old woman in a worn flowered house dress stands at the window of her overheated farmhouse, peering through a pair of binoculars. From here she can see four of the nest boxes around her house. She hates winter. Even though she was born and raised in the house, she has never accepted the fact that half of her life should be spent with snow on the ground, surrounded by a dormant, gray landscape. Each fall she wonders if she will live to see another spring. The weight of the winter just past seemed intolerable, too much to bear. But spring has returned, an unexpected, eye-blinking reprieve of light and activity.

A flash of blue. Yes. She did see it. The male bluebird perches momentarily on a fence post, his bright orange breast defying death, defying winter. By means of the little wooden nest box nearby, the bluebird and the old woman are both home free. Who said she was going to die? Suddenly she is busy. There are some nest boxes that have not yet been cleaned out. The soil in the garden is dry enough to be tilled. She watches the male fly to the nest box and enter. She is glad she got that one cleaned the other day. It is ready for him.

The entrance to the nest box is barely big enough for the small thrush. It has been strategically designed. The old woman built it herself. With a tape she measured off exactly an inch and a half for the diameter of the circular opening — not smaller, not larger. From experience she now knows the meaning of an eighth of an inch when it comes to the girth of a small bird. Smaller than 1⁷⁄₁₆ inches, and a bluebird won't be able to get in the box. Larger than 1⅝ inches, and the starlings will be in there in no time. Of course a house wren and a house sparrow can enter anything that a bluebird can.

NEST
Natural cavities, bluebird houses; lined with grass, weeds

HABITAT
Farmland, gardens, forest edges

EGGS
3–6, pale blue

INCUBATION
12–14 days, by the female

BREEDING RANGE
Eastern half of the United States, in suitable habitat where bluebird houses have been provided

She enjoys keeping an eye on her boxes, checking them every few days. The job takes on a rhythm. Her boxes ring her property and some of her neighbors'. Twenty boxes on the perimeter of 90 acres. She is filled with pride every time she sees a bluebird. Five years ago they were hard to find; now she sees them all summer long. Secretly she feels that they are her bluebirds, and in a way they are. Without her, they would not be there.

Now she watches the male bird with interest and looks to see if his mate has also returned. Very likely he is there ahead of her, checking out the available cavities. The woman steps outside. As if he sees her, he flies up onto a fence post and begins singing, his warbling song announcing the beginning of spring. OK. The answering song in her own mind is simply, "OK." Things are OK. She sits down on the front step and finds herself taking a deep breath. Was she holding it all winter?

A few days later, the woman notices a bluebird, perhaps the same one, displaying at the same box. Without binoculars she can see his head rocking back and forth as he clings to the rim of the entrance. There must be a female nearby. She picks up her glasses and sees that he is holding a piece of dried grass in his beak. He bobs forward and back, sticking his head in and out of the cavity entrance, then looks behind him. Now the woman sees the female bird sitting in the honeysuckle. She seems indifferent. He bobs again, gesturing like a real estate salesman. Does she like the house? Again he feigns entering as if to suggest that this should be her choice. But she seems to be close to opening her little beak and yawning. He droops his wings and spreads his tail feathers, exposing the brilliant blue of his back. Then he pushes off, drops the grass in flight, lands back on the fence post, and sings again. Later, the two birds disappear. The male is most likely showing other possible nest sites to this female and perhaps to others. It could go on for days like this, the male advertising the cavities in his territory, waiting for a female to find one to her liking and accept him as a mate as part of a package deal.

The woman keeps a close eye on the box. It is outside the window that is next to the table where she and her husband eat and where she often reads or types letters. The birds return yet again. Is it the same female? While the woman watches, the female flies over and, for the first time, briefly looks inside the box, then flies back to the fence. The male flutters his wings in excitement. He, in turn, flies to the box and actually goes inside. The woman holds her coffee cup in midair, waiting, watching intently for the next move. Abruptly, the female flies off and disappears, and the male bolts out of the box in pursuit. But in less than an hour, the two birds are back. The woman spots them immediately from her seat on the front step. Again the male flies to the box and enters. She hears him actually singing inside the box! The female flies to the fence post, flies to the box, pokes her head in, and then disappears through the entrance. After a few seconds both birds fly off, but the woman knows that the female's entering the box is most likely a firm declaration that the birds are now a pair.

The woman does not actually see the pair copulate, but over the next couple of weeks the female begins nest-building, dropping to the ground around the nest box for grass. In fact, the female begins building not only in the box outside the window but in two others as well. The male occasionally picks up grass, but the female is the builder. From the beginning, she has seemed to call all the shots, choosily deciding on her mate, making the final decision on which cavity she will occupy, and now building the nest. And when the eggs are laid, she will incubate them herself. The male, on the other hand, has no brood patch and is incapable of true incubation or brooding of the young.

His job is that of defender of the territory, occasional provider of insects to the female on the nest, and often primary provider to the nestlings. He also seems to function simply as a companion to the female, often actually spending nights by her side in the nest box.

Just how much consciousness is behind actions that seem remarkably like our own? During courtship display the female leaves off her brisk efficiency to feign a fluttering, droop-winged, peeping helplessness as the male solicitously feeds her. In this display she seems to embody the helplessness of the future nestlings. Is she, by instinct or deliberation, testing her mate's potential attentiveness? Certainly natural selection, over generations, could favor such a test. But other behavior is harder to explain. Relatively frequently, three or more bluebirds are observed taking care of one brood of nestlings. Sometimes the extra helpers are apparently unrelated adults who seem to spontaneously join the parents in delivering grubs and beetles or removing fecal sacs.

Even in misfortune, the behavior of bluebirds seems strangely familiar. After one male was found dead, his mate was frequently observed sitting side by side with two other females on a fence near the nest. Each female had an insect in her bill, waiting her turn to feed the young. Lawrence Zeleny, founder of the North American Bluebird Society, decribed this scene, noting that the females seemed to be carrying on "friendly bluebird 'conversation.'" I find it amusing and rather charming to think of myself and my friends, nodding and chatting with great big bugs in our mouths, as we attend someone's babies.

Another less serene instance is an even more striking example of bluebird loyalty or instinct. This time, a female bluebird died after pesticides were sprayed near her nest. Fortunately, her nestlings were old enough to survive without brooding, and, as

is common at this stage, the father undertook to rear them alone. Bluebirds usually raise two and sometimes three broods per season. This was a second brood. The father had just embarked on the demanding task of supplying the nestlings with an average of one insect every five minutes from dawn till dusk for almost a month when he was joined by two juvenile males from his previous brood. These young birds were just eight weeks old, having learned only a few weeks before to find insects for themselves. Yet they shared equally with their father the job of bringing insects and regularly carrying away fecal sacs until the nestlings were themselves independent.

Bluebirds frequently nest cooperatively. When one of a pair of bluebirds is killed, other unrelated adults may chip in and help feed young. Even juveniles from a previous brood have been observed feeding nestlings after one parent died.

Eastern bluebirds winter in the southeastern U.S., Mexico, and Central America. While insects form the bulk of their diet in the summer months, holly, sumac, and other berries are critical for their survival in the winter.

With instances of apparent altruism in nature, there is much speculation as to what might be the motive other than simple generosity. A shortage of potential nest sites seems to be one condition that encourages cooperation, and the "altruism" tends to help the species as a whole. This is the case with the red-cock-aded woodpecker, also a cooperative breeder. Certainly among the bluebirds there is an increasingly desperate lack of nest sites. Traditionally, bluebirds nested in hollow trees. But with the arrival of the chain saw and an increased fear of lawsuits due to falling limbs, trees are quickly manicured, and dead wood is hard to find. On farms, wooden fence posts, which commonly offered hollows for the birds, have generally been replaced by metal. With the advent of "broad spectrum" pesticides that kill all insects in their range and not just targeted pests, orchards, once popular territories of bluebirds, are now wisely shunned. Of course the very insects these sprays kill are the mainstay of the bluebirds. Woodlots and hedgerows, once common features of traditional family farms, are often eliminated as farms are absorbed by larger operations. With them go nesting cavities.

Another considerable threat to bluebirds exists in their winter range. While bluebirds feed almost exclusively on insects in the warm months, they live almost entirely on berries from late summer until spring. American holly was once an important source of berries, its fruit softening after other berries have been eaten. But this valuable wild plant is now aggressively harvested for Christmas decorations. Other types of berries that once flourished in undeveloped areas have become scarce as human uses have been found for one wild place after another. In their southern winter range, bluebirds have traditionally faced periodic killing storms, but in recent decades, with the added stress of inadequate food supplies, the species no longer seems to bounce back. If people who live within the bluebirds' winter range plant berries for the birds eat, their chances of survival rise significantly.

The female bluebird in the old woman's yard spends five days building her grass nest. She begins laying eggs soon after the nest is finished, one egg each morning. The old woman goes out one afternoon to check her nest boxes and finds that this one now contains five delicate blue eggs. The woman has never yet looked at a nest of bluebird eggs without being brought up short by their pure blue color. She pauses and then quickly shuts up the nest box so the female can return.

Several days later, on her way to the garden, the woman sees a house sparrow dart into the nest box. She curses and hurries over. As she starts to open the nest, the sparrow flies out. The woman braces for the unpleasant sight inside, but she can never be quite ready. She lifts up the side wall of the nest box. The sparrow has nearly filled the box with grass and dead leaves and twigs. Sandwiched between this mass and the bluebird nest in the bottom of the box is the bright blue wing of a bluebird. The woman reaches in and begins pulling out the mass of nest material, uncovering the body of the male, his head severely pecked by the sparrow. The five blue eggs fall to the ground with the grass.

The house sparrow was introduced intentionally into North America because it was considered pretty and useful in controlling insects. Fifty years later, the species had spread across the United States. It competes aggressively for cavities bluebirds might use.

Starlings, house sparrows, and house wrens have made it nearly impossible for bluebirds to nest successfully without frequent human monitoring. House sparrows, also known as English sparrows, are actually weaver finches, introduced from Europe in 1851. Since that time they have spread thoughout most of North America, wreaking havoc on the lives of small cavity nesters. In 1890, starlings came on the North American scene, also introduced from Europe. A well-meaning admirer of Shakespeare, in an effort to have all the birds mentioned in Shakespeare take up residence around him, released 60 starlings

The entrance to a bluebird house must measure between 1 ⁷/₁₆ inches and 1 ½ inches. This seems exacting, but an entrance even a sixteenth of an inch larger will admit starlings to the nest box.

in New York's Central Park in 1890 and 40 more in 1891. These birds wasted no time in getting settled. That first summer, one pair nested in the eaves of the American Museum of Natural History. By the 1950s, the starling was reported to have made it to California, and nested throughout the rest of United States and southern Canada. On this continent, starlings are even tougher competitors for bluebirds than house sparrows, not only killing adults and throwing young and eggs out of their nests, but descending in hordes to quickly gulp down the wild berries that once sustained bluebirds till spring. The house wren, a tiny bird much adored by those who have had the pleasure of watching it nest, is another menace. The male house wren, in his overzealous enthusiasm to supply a nest for his mate, will fill all available cavities in his territory full of twigs and aggressively defend them from intruders. Should a pair of bluebirds already be using a cavity, the tiny wren will often slip in when the adults are gone and destroy the eggs or young nestlings.

The old woman keeps an eye on the box, persistently removing the nest materials of the sparrows each time they return to build. Finally, another pair of bluebirds appears and takes up occupancy. The woman knows that the female is probably not from the previous pair. Generally, if a pair succeeds in fledging young from a site, they will remain monogamous and nest there again that season. But if for any reason young are not fledged from a particular site, the adults or surviving adult usually move elsewhere. As the summer goes on, five more eggs are laid in the box. Though the eggs are laid one per day, incubation is not commenced until the clutch is complete. Thus the eggs will hatch at approximately the same time. One day, seeing the male arrive with a soft grub in his beak, the woman knows that the

eggs have hatched. At first, the nestlings are fed soft insects, the male gathering most of the food and delivering it to his mate, who actually feeds it to the young. Later, they both begin delivering crickets, grasshoppers, beetles — sterner stuff, with exoskeletons and legs. Without even looking in the box, the woman can tell the approximate age of a brood by this change in diet. Another clue is that when the chicks are young, the adults go inside the box to feed them, but when they are older, the adults hang on the rim of the entrance and just stick in their heads.

When the young are not quite a week old, the female stops feeding them and moves to another box to build a new nest. The male takes over full time, characteristically perching on low shrubs and fences, surveying the ground until he spots an insect, then darting down, snatching it, and winging off to the nest. The nestlings grow rapidly. On the 18th day after hatching, they begin leaving the box. Like most cavity nesters, the fledglings can fly adequately on their first attempt. While a bird that nests in the open, like the robin, is more likely to produce young that wind up on the ground wondering how to fly after their first attempt, cavity nesters seem generally capable of flight without first testing their wings. The old woman has carefully positioned her nest boxes so there is a shrub or tree within 75 or 100 yards to collect each brood as it fledges. She watches with satisfaction from her window as nature cooperates with her. Five fledglings, their breasts dappled with the spots of the thrush family, clamber up through the branches of a honeysuckle, and the woman knows all the more surely that to witness this faltering ascent is perhaps the best reason she was put on this earth.

Bluebird populations have declined by 90 percent during the twentieth century. Felling dead trees and removing dead branches from living trees has eliminated critical nesting cavities.

House Wren

NEST
Natural cavities, old woodpecker
holes, birdhouses; made of twigs
lined with grasses, feathers, hair,
plant fibers, miscellaneous objects
HABITAT
Farmland, gardens, open woods
EGGS
6–8, white, densely covered with
reddish speckles
INCUBATION
12–15 days, by the female
BREEDING RANGE
In appropriate habitat throughout most of the United States
except the far South

The air is warm in the cabin. It passes freely through chinks between the logs, but it does not cool the man who lies in bed in a
dim corner of the room. He is not asleep. He is simply waiting
out sickness.

It is mid-April. Bird songs make a mockery of disease. From
a single window, bright light pours in, light that seems to bring
the yellow-green of leaves right into the dark cabin. Somewhere
close by, a male house wren sings over and over. As is typical of
his species, his song is nervous, repetitious. But for the man,
who has nothing else to occupy his time, each note stands out as
a gift. He follows the bird's movements with his ears, then suddenly he does not hear the song. He waits for it to begin again.
He hears distant wrens. Perhaps it has flown off. He closes his
eyes and dozes.

But no sooner has the man drifted off than he is brought
back, alert for the first time in a week. He has heard the barest
click or scratch within the room. He does not move his head but
strains with his eyes to see in the direction of his desk by the
window. The window is closed, yet hopping past it, on the inside, a house wren is making its way rather incautiously across
the bookshelf. The man is stunned. So little has happened to
him in a week's time that he forgets to breathe for a moment.
His heart pounds as if a bear had entered the cabin.

The little wren seems to know exactly where it is going. It
hops down onto the writing surface of the desk and right into a
pigeonhole that has been left vacant of envelopes or pens. It disappears into the dark rectangle and reappears, disappears again,
reappears, and hops to the upper shelf of the desk. It hops again
to the writing surface, back into the pigeonhole, then suddenly

flies across the room and is gone. The man lies back thinking about the wren until he dozes.

He is awakened by the wren again. This time it carries a stick in its beak. It tries to put the stick into the pigeonhole crosswise, but the stick is too long to fit. After only two tries, the wren turns its head and feeds the stick in sideways. It flies off across the room but is back in minutes with a new twig. And so begins what will stretch into a week of nest building. The male comes

House wrens have been found nesting in unusual places: the pockets of scarecrows, cow skulls, tin cans, teapots, old boots, hats, the rear axle of an auto that was actually driven. (The wrens rode along, and the eggs successfully hatched.) Wrens also may use unusual materials. One nest contained 52 hairpins, 188 nails, 4 tacks, 13 staples, 10 pins, 4 pieces of pencil lead, 11 safety pins, 6 paper clips, 52 wires, 1 buckle, 2 hooks, and 3 garter fasteners.

and goes, singing outside near the cabin, leaving to feed, and returning with more twigs.

Then one morning the man awakens to find the male, his tail cocked stiffly forward, his wings quivering, watching a female inspect the nest. She hops onto the writing surface, then into the pigeonhole, pushing past the twigs, hops out, hops to the upper shelf, hops back to the writing surface. Then, apparently having accepted the male as her mate, she begins to throw the twigs out of the pigeonhole onto the man's week-old correspondence. The male cocks his tail even farther forward, his wings quivering with his excitement at her acceptance.

The female returns with twigs of her own choosing, virtually identical to those selected by the male. In fact, she even picks up some of the sticks she has thrown out onto the desk. For the next several days, both birds build. When it seems to the man that the pigeonhole cannot possibly hold another twig, the female returns with some fluffy white plant down in her beak, a sign that she will soon lay her eggs.

The first egg appears pale salmon-colored, with minute, cinnamon brown speckles fused over the white surface of the egg. The next egg, laid the following day, has more white between dots. The female wren comes and goes, checking her eggs and leaving to feed. The speckles on the third egg are wreathed slightly toward the broad end of the egg. The egg of the fourth day is pink, like the first. And so the clutch of six eggs is laid, one a day, each one a fresh surprise to the man who makes his way across the room to inspect the nest each noon after the wren is gone.

On the sixth morning, the wren enters the pigeonhole and stays. Incubation has begun. The female always takes the night shift, but during the day the male takes his turns. The man feels a warm sense of anticipation as he watches them come and go.

This story is based on a true account of fairly typical wren behavior. Colonel S.T. Walker wrote in 1889, "I was sick at the time, and watched the whole proceeding from the laying of the first stick to the conclusion. The nest was placed in one of the pigeonholes of my desk, and the birds effected an entrance to the room through sundry cracks in the log cabin."

I don't know what illness the man had, but I wonder if he couldn't have gotten up sooner than 47 days after the little wren first made its appearance in the room. I think he wanted to wait for that day when one of the wrens first returned to the nest with an insect in its beak. And once that happened, he probably began counting trips and couldn't stop. Over a thousand trips a day, often two trips a minute.

During his illness he was able to keep this log of the nesting cycle of his wrens:

Nest begun	April 15th
Nest completed and first egg laid	April 27th
Last egg laid	May 3rd
Began incubation	May 4th
Hatching completed	May 18th
Young began to fly	May 27th
Young left the nest	June 1st
Total time occupied	47 days

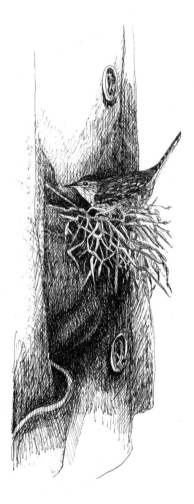

7

Cup Nests

~

One day not long ago, I stood in the rain watching my five-year-old son climb a hawthorn tree to retrieve a small nest. This was his own idea, and though I was getting soaked, I did not want to interrupt his journey. As he progressed carefully up through the spiny branches, I eyed the distance he could fall, my mind conjuring up horrible images of him lying in a heap under the tree. Yet while I wanted to ask him to forget the nest, I stood, with rain running down my face, savoring my son's determination. At the end, however, the branches grew too weak to support a small boy's weight. The nest remained out of his reach, and I felt fresh admiration for the effectiveness of the cup nest.

The female robin builds a nest of twigs and grasses, which she binds with mud and shapes from the inside with her breast. A soft inner lining of fine grasses pushed into the mud cradles the eggs.

American Robin

NEST
Woven foundation of twigs, grass,
or string worked into a mud cup
with inner lining of fine grasses;
built on branch or in buildings
HABITAT
Cities, farms, gardens, open
woods
EGGS
3–5, blue
INCUBATION
12–14 days, by the female
BREEDING RANGE
Throughout the United States
and Canada

Hermit thrush

A child opens the kitchen door and walks in proudly carrying a bird's nest to show his mother. It would, of course, have been awkward if not impossible for him to walk in with a heron's bulky, loosely assembled nest or an eagle's massive nest or a tern's nonexistent nest or a grebe's floating nest. But a robin's nest seems made for a child to find and cherish and place on a shelf in the bedroom where it can, without disintegrating, gather dust for years. Indeed, the robin seems to be a bird perfectly designed for human awareness. It is the classic bird, builder of the classic nest. Most Americans, I suspect, can identify a robin. Robins hop along in easy view of humans throughout North America. They are at home on the tundra, at 12,000-foot elevations in the Canadian Rockies, along the ocean in arid Baja, and of course, right on our lawns. On trips to fairly exotic parts of the continent, I have reached hurriedly for my binoculars to identify a passing bird and been disappointed to find it was "just a robin."

But I have made a conscious effort to avoid taking robins for granted. I simply have to remember that they belong to the thrush family, among the most beautiful and poignant of birds. I was not aware of thrushes until I moved to New England. I lived for a couple of years in a little cabin, sleeping on the second floor with a little door open all summer out onto a balcony that looked into the treetops. It was here that I met the wood thrush and the elusive hermit thrush, state bird of Vermont. The song of the wood thrush typified all that I hoped Vermont represented. It sounded like the easy, relaxed movement of a porch swing. I imagined an old woman, one foot down to the floor of the porch, gently pushing, keeping the swing in motion. There had been no such sound in Southern California. I used to lie in

my treetop bed in the summer, with the wealth of leaves soothing my dry soul, thinking that there could be no other place on
earth as luxurious as this. When, occasionally, the hermit thrush
added his fluid, mysterious call, I was convinced.

But now I am back in California, growing to know the
forests of the Northwest that I visited too infrequently as a child.
I did not know, in those early visits, that there were thrushes
here, the Swainson's and the varied, even the hermit. To stand
alone in a redwood forest, amid trees that seem to begin at the
sky and enlarge downward to root massively at one's feet, living
monuments to age and permanence, is one of those reliably balancing experiences that should be enjoyed by all Americans. The
experience is not complete, however, until as one stands there
silently, one is startled by the single-note, drawn-out call of a
varied thrush. After the call, there is silence, and then the call is
uttered again at a different pitch, and then silence again, and
then a third pitch, on and on, as if, in the cathedral-like space
and time of the redwood forest, the bird had eternity to tune his
song.

In our yard we have an old windbreak of Monterey cypress,
huge trees planted, perhaps, when our house was built over a
century ago. We are honored to host Swainson's thrushes, which
seem to prefer such established cover as these trees or the dark
spruce woods on the edge of town. In spring, as I work outside, I
call to my children when I hear a thrush. "Listen. What bird is
that?" By now they know. And I suppose they get tired of my
telling them, over and over, that no matter where they live when
they are older, this song will always remind them of this place,
these big dark trees, this old glassed-in greenhouse, this tree fort
with its litter of barn owl pellets, this big old barn knocked
askew by earthquakes. I know, because I have a friend who no
longer lives among trees that attract thrushes. She comes to my

Varied thrush

house and abruptly stops and listens and remembers all that was best in her childhood.

So all of this charged-up feeling I take to the experience of seeing a robin. When I say to myself, "This isn't simply a robin; this is a thrush," I see the bird as more ephemeral. Its red breast seems more shimmering, its song more flutelike. I watch it on a lawn and wonder about pesticides and herbicides. The compelling thing about thrushes is that, except for the bluebird and the robin, they are rarely seen. The downward spiraling song of the veery, the isolated notes of the varied thrush, the moody song of the wood thrush, and the mysterious voice of the hermit, all seem to come from heaven. But the robin, with its *cheerup, cheerily, cheerup* uttered in plain view in a garden, is one of the most valuable of life's everyday treasures.

Actually, robins were not always so common. Like the barn owl, the robin has benefited from the settling of North America. Robins are not adapted to deep forest, and even the plains of the Midwest were once too dry and scarce in earthworms to support robins. But settlers moved west, clutching axes, irrigation pipe, and potted plants hosting earthworms for their future gardens. Things got even better with the spread of the suburbs. As nearly as anyone can guess, the robin is happiest in that ultimate of civilized settings, a nice neighborhood of little houses surrounded by trimmed lawns and shade trees with a golf course or a park nearby. In such a setting there is little reason for conflict between robins and humans, and while robins that breed in remote areas are generally shy of people, the suburban robin boldly hops by in plain view, building a nest that is one of the most easily located of any bird's.

If it is spring and you see robins, they are most likely nesting or about to nest. Robins are among the first birds to arrive on

their breeding grounds, the males preceding the females by a few days. During the winter, the majority of robins roost communally in large flocks in southern states. With the arrival of spring, flocks of males head north, dispersing as the birds near their natal areas, often returning to the exact territories in which they nested the year before. Even if you have robins in your area year-round, it is likely that your winter robins head farther north in spring and are replaced by a new batch from farther south, the whole population shifting north when temperatures rise above 37 degrees.

One can tell a male robin from a female by his more intense red breast and his darker brown head and tail. These colors, set against the bright green of a lawn that is about to receive its first spring trim, are the classic stuff of kids' paintings. As the ground warms, earthworms move up from below, and when they begin to emerge, robins pull them out of the ground. Contrary to what I was taught in elementary school, a robin standing on the grass and cocking his head sideways is not listening for worms but watching for them. He cocks his head simply because his eyes are on the sides of his head. Male robins periodically engage

In winter, it is not unusual to see robins taking turns at a birdbath or hopping together on a lawn. Once the breeding season begins, however, they lose their tolerance for close contact.

each other in combat over feeding territories. Having lost much of their winter tolerance for one another's presence, they repel each other like magnets with a reverse field of energy, pushing without touching and actively chasing until their territories are established.

It is said that robins are landowners first and lovers second. This is true of many birds that are "site-specific." Their instinct is to return to a particular place, generally near the place they were hatched, but not to a particular mate. Since both members of a previously mated pair return to the same spot the next year, about one out of eight robins re-pair with a previous mate. If the male of a mated pair is driven off by a stronger suitor, the female generally accepts the new male. Because it is seldom seen, robin courtship and mating are suspected to be minimal, the female wasting no time getting on with building her nest. The male's song, in fact, while it is uttered during courtship and territorial defense, seems loudest and most exuberant just before the hatching of his family.

To encourage robins to nest in your area, it is helpful to provide several key elements. First, robins need horizontal surfaces to support their nests. In the absence of tree limbs or suitable ledges on man-made structures such as houses or outbuildings, you might construct sturdy shelves six inches wide and eight inches long, five to twenty feet off the ground, that are protected from rain. The birds will also need a pan of mud or clay, or a flooded area of dirt kept muddy during nest-building, and cloth strips and string and yarn, less than a foot long so robins will not become entangled. You can tell that a female is engaged in nest-building by the line of mud that shows on her breast as she flies back and forth picking up building materials.

A robin builds a statant nest; that is, one that is supported from below, as compared to a suspended nest, which is supported from the rim or sides. Thus the free-standing sides of the nest must be strong enough to contain the eggs and nestlings and the nine- to eleven-inch female robin while she is in the nest for incubation and brooding. This strength is achieved with mud incorporated into the nest wall. Construction occurs in roughly three stages. Imagine a typical female robin who has chosen a nest site on the branch of an apple tree. First, she and her mate begin assembling grass, straw, leaves, rootlets, and string, which she weaves into a firm foundation, periodically standing or squatting in the center and pressing with her breast and wings to mold the material to the contour of her body. Next she returns to the nest with pellets of mud in her beak and sticks these onto the nest's inner walls. She then gets into the nest and pushes with her feet, rotating her breast around to pat the plastered walls into a smooth bowl. She then gathers fine grasses, which she presses into the damp mud, cementing a soft lining into place.

If the weather is dry, building may have to be suspended until rain makes mud. One robin was observed, however, bringing water in her beak to a dusty area to make mud. Another was observed doing the reverse, taking dirt in her beak and flying to water. Deviations in building materials may occur in extreme climatic conditions. In Maine, robins have been observed using moss in their nests for insulation. In areas with high winds, wiry little rootlets may be woven in for greater strength.

Two days after the nest is complete, one sky blue egg is visible in the bowl of the nest. Thrushes lay some of the most beautiful of all bird eggs, and nearly everyone is familiar with the color called robin's-egg blue. The shell is a rich blue-green lying on the muted yellow-green of the fine grass. Each morning there is another egg, but not until the clutch of four is complete does the female stay on the nest and begin incubation. Thus all of the

The nestlings of robins and other songbirds are altricial. The word altricial *comes from Latin, "to nourish." Altricial hatchlings are naked or have very little down, their eyes are closed, and they are unable to leave the nest. At the opposite extreme are* precocial *nestlings, a word that derives from the same Latin root as* precocious. *A typical precocial chick is that of the domestic chicken.*

nestlings will hatch within 24 hours of each other. Once incubation begins, the female leaves the nest only to feed, about five or ten minutes out of each hour. During these intervals the eggs are left exposed, but the male and female robin are always close by and immediately return to the nest if danger threatens. Several times each day the female robin hops to the rim of her nest and, with her beak, turns each of the eggs. As is the case with all bird eggs, the yolk must be periodically shifted within the egg so that it will not adhere to the inside of the shell.

Like a pound cake recipe, the intervals of development that result in an independent fledgling robin are easy to remember: approximately two weeks of incubation time, two weeks of development in the nest, and two weeks spent off the nest but still dependent on parental support. There is probably no baby bird so pathetically helpless as a newly hatched robin. Altricial hatchlings are among the ugliest infants in the animal kingdom, with their naked, bright pink skin; grotesquely huge black eyes visible through closed transluscent lids; long, skinny necks; and disproportionate, swollen stomachs, like those of starving children. When the parent robins return to the nest with food, the slight jiggling of the nest causes the baby birds to instantly throw open their beaks, revealing garish orange throat linings that clash with the nestlings' pink bodies. This orange has its purpose, however, instantly prompting the parents' instinct to "bill-thrust" — to jam soft grubs, spiders, and caterpillars down the throats of their young about every five to ten minutes from dawn till dusk.

The change that takes place in the nestlings over the next two weeks is astounding. Consuming a total of three pounds of food, each nestling increases its body weight by 1,000 percent. It is no wonder that robin nestlings kept in captivity frequently starve to death. Few humans have the time to provide a single nestling with the equivalent of 14 feet of earthworm per day!

And of course the amount of waste is proportionate, keeping the parents busy transporting fecal sacs and other waste on their return trips. So eager are the robins to remove any organic debris that might be a source of disease that one poor nestling was flown over a campground and dropped. Closer inspection led campers to surmise that a parent robin had brought home a piece of liver, which now lay half in and half out of the nestling's beak. On the next trip to the nest, the parent snatched the liver in its beak, unaware that its baby was connected, and discarded them both, baby-and-bathwater style.

After little more than a week in the nest, the baby robins have all their feathers. That they are thrushes is apparent in the beautiful speckling of their breasts. While the bluebird and robin and varied thrush are all brilliantly colored birds with bright plumage, the elusive hermit thrush, wood thrush, veery, and Swainson's thrush are all camouflaged by their speckles. The robin nestlings' speckling helps protect them while they are learning to fly.

On about day six, robins develop fear. Before this they can be handled easily by humans, but after the first week they are terrified. By comparison, ducklings, which are precocial, learn fear within 24 hours. Humans, on the other hand, learn fear at the age of six to nine months. It is hard to say whether being fearful is any help when the nestlings, at a little less than two weeks of age, propel themselves from the nest to the ground. Though their parents stand guard and continue to feed the fledglings, they are little protection against a determined domestic cat, dog, owl, raccoon, skunk, or squirrel looking for a meal. Since the nestlings will be incapable of actual flight for

Juvenile robins look more like their other thrush relatives than they do their own parents. Their brown, dappled plumage helps protect them during the period after they leave the nest but have not yet learned to fly.

several more days, they are unable to return to the nest for safety.

Given this odd, unprotected interval in robin existence, one might wonder how robins have continued to increase in numbers over the last century. While robins have a potential life span of 10 or more years, the actual average lifespan of a robin is one and a half years. Thirty percent of robin eggs never hatch. Another 30 percent of the nestlings die before they leave the nest. Only 7 percent live to the end of their first year. Just 1 – 2 percent live to three years of age. On the other hand, each pair of robins generally produces two to three broods per season, totaling eight to twelve eggs. If each of these eggs were to eventually result in an adult robin, at the end of 30 years a single hypothetical pair of robins would have 1.2 billion trillion descendants, far more than could fit on the surface of the Earth if they stood shoulder to shoulder!

There are, however, significant dangers to robins that are within our control. The first of these is human negligence in the control of the domestic cat. It is estimated that there are approximately 55 million cats in the contiguous United States. Perhaps 20 percent of these either do not go outside or are too old to hunt, leaving 44 million on the prowl. One could conservatively estimate that at least one in ten of these cats will catch a songbird on any given day. This computes to the nationwide loss of more than 4 million songbirds daily.

Another danger in our own backyards arises from the use of herbicides and pesticides. Because robins and their nestlings depend for much of the year on food that comes from our lawns and flower beds, we must ask ourselves what we are putting in our soil and on our leaves that will be concentrated in the bodies of earthworms and other insects and then further concentrated

NESTLINGS *(opposite)*

1 *Killdeer*

2 *Pied-billed grebe*

3 *Ruby-throated hummingbird*

4 *Great egret*

5 *American robin*

6 *Wood duck*

7 *Red-eyed vireo*

8 *Brown-headed cowbird*

9 *Common murre*

10 *Bald eagle*

11 *Great horned owl*

1

2

3

4

5

6

7

8

9

10

11

in the bodies of robins. Usually we do not find the robins we kill. This is part of the problem. Certainly there are few people who, faced with a yard full of dead birds, would not quickly change their gardening practices or give up gardening altogether! But poisons are often stored, unassimilated, in fat reserves. It is not until those fat reserves are called upon because a bird is near starvation that a pesticide may claim another victim, many miles away from the pretty lawn where the poison was administered. I think of my mother's perfect garden, surrounded by houses with other perfect gardens. When I was a child, there were many songbirds in the neighborhood and an abundance of little golden butterflies. Now the garden seems to belong just to her. If she were given a choice, I know she would prefer to have the birds and butterflies back. But their absence is the result of many people's choices over many years.

It is estimated that housecats in the United States kill 4 million songbirds a day.

Cliff Swallow

Inside one of many little clay flasks stuck high up on a granite rock face, two birds await the arrival of an early summer thunderstorm. The female has five white speckled eggs tucked beneath her. Her mate rests in the entrance to the nest, blocking the light with his body as he watches the storm darken the river valley below. The undersides of the approaching thunderheads are fused to the land with a deep blue-gray band of falling rain. The erasure of boundaries between Earth and sky give the appearance that beneath these clouds, all stops have been pulled and anything goes. The last of the swallows leave off swooping and retreat to their nests. In the eerie light under the fierce blue clouds, the clay nests, stacked one on top of the other on the cliff face, look too fragile and porous to withstand a rainstorm. They look like unfired earthenware, with disconcertingly little evidence of any grass or twig reinforcement protruding from the clay.

The wind arrives first, bringing the rain on with a blast. Thunder and lightning strike simultaneously. The valley below is instantly obscured by the downpour, and the only sound is rain pounding on stone. The male swallow pulls his head in, and in half-light, the two wait. Above, below, and alongside them, the other pairs of swallows do the same. The pelting is steady, but no nests collapse. No families are suddenly thrust into oozing and undignified landslides of mud and eggs. The walls, the ceilings, the floors hold strong.

Then, as abruptly as it began, the rain ends. The thunderheads move on, and the outlines of their crisp, billowing towers become visible again. The thunder rumbles distantly, already miles away. Now the only sound is of water trickling off the cliff face. In the round entrances to the nests, heads reappear, each

bird poised to push off into air momentarily. Remarkably, not only is the swallow colony intact, but the rock immediately around the nests is actually dry, protected by overhangs that are barely noticeable in fair weather.

But how, since their nests must be built when the weather is dry, did the swallows know the direction the wind would take and which surfaces would be protected? There is no evidence of trial and error. There are no remains of nests ruthlessly eliminated by previous storms. Perhaps the birds build when the rock face seems dry but retains telltale moisture that is a tipoff about future storm conditions. But what if no storms occur before nest-building? Have generations of experience given the birds an instinctive sense about where to build?

The colony is built in an elegant honeycomb design. Roughly hexagonal where it is attached to the rock, each nest is generally offset half a step from the one above, like the cells in a beehive. This design not only allows for maximum space inside the nest in proportion to the amount of mud used, it allows a maximum number of nests to be built on the sheltered surface of the cliff. Perhaps even more critically, it keeps the excrement of the nestlings, as they defecate out the door of a nest, from landing on the roof of the nest immediately below.

Occasionally cliff swallows do make mistakes, however. A paper with the dismal title "Violation of Ideal Nest Placement: Cliff Swallows Entombed by Their Own Excrement" describes the fate of a pair of swallows whose neighbors built directly below their nest, literally setting the stage for a wall of excrement to build up in front of the door of the innocent swallows above. It is normal for adults to feed nestlings after the first few days without actually entering the nest, and apparently neither of the adults was alarmed as the wall grew. By fledging time, the little prisoners could protrude only their heads from the nest. Fortunately, the author of the paper intervened, climbing up to chip away the guano. One nestling had already died, but the other three fledged successfully.

Occasionally, the nests of swallows are deliberately used as tombs by the birds. Another observer once noticed several swallows all busily adding mud to the same nest. Closer inspection revealed that a swallow had died inside, probably of natural causes. Since the birds were not capable of removing the corpse, they simply brought mud and walled it in. The burial may have prevented the spread of disease.

The cliff swallow regards the slightest irregularity of surface as an invitation to start building. Often this toehold is provided by the vertical mud tube nest of the mud dauber wasp, which is even better equipped than the swallow to wedge mud into tiny crevices. On this foundation, both male and female swallows add mud, dropping to hover at the edge of a puddle, often holding their feet clear of the mud as they scoop up beakfuls and roll them into balls. Like the adobe bricks of the Mission San Juan Capistrano, the little daubs are applied one by one, first in the hexagon that outlines the perimeter of the nest and then one on top of the other till the nest's flask shape is complete. The bottleneck entrance is aimed slightly downward as an extra precaution against rain and predators. A flock of cliff swallows will build nests at the same time. Often they build in the morning, then take a break to swoop for insects while the mud dries. They periodically return to the nests to check on how the mud is hardening, and eventually resume their work. Depending on the weather, the nests may take from three days to two weeks to complete.

While many of our birds are in some degree of decline, both cliff and particularly barn swallows are actually increasing in numbers. Although some fastidious farmers discourage nesting by painting surfaces or even removing nests, the rise of the automobile has improved nesting conditions for swallows. The construction of superhighways, with their many bridges and culverts, has afforded new habitat throughout North America. Perhaps the greatest threat to cliff swallows has been the English sparrow, or house sparrow, introduced to North America in the late 1800s. This bird will often usurp a newly established swallow colony, pitching eggs and nestlings to the ground and then filling each nest with additional grass for the sparrow families. On

the other hand, cowbirds, nest parasites that have reduced populations of other birds that build open nests, rarely intrude in swallow colonies.

At the colony on the granite rock face, the rain has stopped. One by one the swallows push from their entrances and soar through the gorge, stretching their wings, waiting for insects to join them in air. The flight is effortless, as if the wind took pleasure in the birds. Swallows, along with swifts, expend half the effort of other passerines in flight. They eat, drink, and even bathe in midair, rarely coming to rest when not nesting except to hover, half alighted, while they gather mud for their nests, and momentarily for copulation. While swallows have been found with crops full of berries, their usual diet is almost entirely made up of insects.

It has been estimated that a typical brood of four to five nestlings requires 900 insects each day for the three weeks until they leave the nest, for a total of nearly 20,000 weevils, chinch bugs, grasshoppers, beetles, mosquitoes, and other insects. Picture a heap of this many insects killed by an electronic bug zapper or a poison-filled trap, and it is easy to appreciate the value of these beautiful birds, which give us so much more than just insect control.

Barn Swallow

Though barn swallows and cliff swallows may nest in the same barn, they tend to occupy slightly different niches. Cliff swallows have a slightly wilder lifestyle, foraging and perching higher, flying farther for their mud. Barn swallows, on the other hand, are more likely to take mud right out of the barnyard. Cliff swallows seem to be less adapted to human interference. If the barn doors are shut, for instance, barn swallows will attempt to find an alternate route, but cliff swallows will usually abandon their nests. While barn swallows once nested in natural settings, as the cliff swallow still does, they now nest almost exclusively in man-made structures, generally choosing a horizontal shelf for their open, half-cup-shaped nests. While cliff swallows are an exclusively American species, barn swallows, one of the most widespread species of birds on Earth, have had a long association with humans throughout not only North America but Europe and Asia as well. Barn swallows appear in the myths of ancient Greece, China, Japan, and Europe. One German farmer said that he was taught that barns housing swallows would never be struck by lightning, and that if a farmer killed a swallow his cows' milk would go bad. Like San Juan Capistrano, California, the city of Beijing, China is called the "city of the swallows." Songs of welcome for returning swallows survive from ancient Greece. And in Japan, swallow nests are considered shrines for children.

Barn swallow nests are among the easiest to find and observe. If you see two swallows perched close together on a wire, they are almost surely a mated pair. If they fly down to the ground and then swoop into an open building, they are most likely collecting mud and carrying it to a nest in progress. You need only follow the birds inside to find the nest. When the nest

NEST
Half-circular cup made of mud pellets with straw, lined with feathers; plastered to the wall of a building or other structure, occasionally to a cliff face

HABITAT
Open countryside, especially near farms; rural towns

EGGS
4–7, white with brown spots

INCUBATION
13–17 days, by both parents

BREEDING RANGE
Throughout most of the United States and Canada, northern Mexico

Barn swallows can be encouraged to nest by the construction of a small shelf a few inches below the ceiling of a barn, outbuilding, or porch. A simple, flat shelf that can be scraped off can be placed under the nest to catch droppings. Barn swallows may use the same nest year after year.

is completed, you may see the lining protruding over the edge; while both cliff swallows and barn swallows line their nests with grass and feathers, barn swallows especially favor white chicken feathers. A few days after the nest is built, four to five eggs will be laid. In about two weeks, when both parents begin actively flying back and forth again, you can be sure that the nestlings have hatched and are being fed. When excrement starts landing on the ground below the nest and the adults with food hover in air to avoid being mobbed by their aggressive offspring, you know that the nestlings are approximately a week old. When, about three weeks after hatching, you look up and see the nest bulging with wide-mouthed youngsters, it is clearly time for fledging, though the young birds will try to wedge themselves back in the nest at night for a while.

It is possible to attract barn swallows to a building with the simple addition of small shelves a few inches below the ceiling. A wider shelf built below the nest will collect droppings and is easily cleaned with a flat shovel. Once occupied, nests may be relined with mud by the birds and used year after year. One nest was still in use 20 years after its initial construction.

Both cliff and barn swallows winter in the southern hemisphere. While Eurasian barn swallows move south into Africa, North American swallows of both species migrate to South America. Indeed, some barn swallows have the longest migration route of any North American land bird, traveling 7,000 miles from the Yukon to Brazil and Argentina. While the clearing of rain forest threatens to eliminate many of our most treasured songbirds, neither swallow is a forest species.

American Dipper

I have two favorite memories from elementary school. The first is from fourth grade, when an art teacher taught us how to draw a giant sequoia — something I instantly realized I very much wanted to know. Like the Little Prince with his hat, I can still draw this tree, and I still remember the rush of excitement I felt the first time it appeared beneath my pencil.

The second experience was when another teacher placed on my desk a mimeographed one-page description of the "water ouzel," or American dipper. Like the first experience, this one felt sudden and unexpected. So much of school is spent learning the answers to questions we have not yet asked, that it is often startling when one of our budding passions is actually touched. Often these passions are so new we cannot even yet identify them. But to this day I vividly remember the color of the mimeograph ink, and the single-spaced, hard-to-read text.

This little purple tract described a songbird with typical perching feet who dove under rushing mountain streams as it looked for insects. The paper told me that this bird had an extra set of transparent eyelids that worked like goggles underwater. I now know that this was not exactly right. Most birds have a third inner eyelid, called the nictitating membrane, which commonly protects the eye from drying during flight and which in some diving birds is equipped with a special lenslike window for improved vision underwater. But there is debate over whether the dipper closes its nictitating membrane while underwater. It is agreed, however, that the eyelid, which the dipper blinks much more often than most birds, functions to clear the eyes of spray and may even help to camouflage the bird, the flashing motion blending with the sparkle of a moving stream. Fine points aside, however, for me the paper was a window on the larger topic of adaptation. An underwater songbird with goggles! Not long after, I spotted the word *ecology* on the cover of a volume of my father's Time-Life nature series, and I announced to him that I thought I would become an "ecologist."

It is not hard to find a dipper in the mountains of the West. One need merely sit by a stream and wait. The dipper religiously follows its watercourse, taking no shortcuts across land but zigzagging right, left, up, down with the stream's channel, zipping close by anyone sitting in its way. Like the kingfisher, the dipper has a linear territory, a segment of stream or river that it combs for insects, both above and below the surface. I have always felt that the loon is the most purely aquatic of birds, but this strange little songbird, with its wiry, unwebbed feet, seems equally one with the water, not even seeming to notice when it changes elements. One moment it is foraging on shore; the next it walks right into the water and, without hesitating to catch its breath, completely submerges and walks upstream. Or it may fly in and out of the water, flapping its wings beneath the surface and rising to become airborne once more without seeming to miss a beat.

This fluidity is made possible by several adaptations that are particularly remarkable in a songbird. One of these is the dipper's large uropygial gland. Most birds have a uropygial gland.

Anyone who has prepared a whole chicken for roasting has seen this gland above the tail and perhaps pivoted the knife point to cut it out. While this gland may have other uses, its main function is in waterproofing the feathers. While preening, birds put their heads back, wipe their bills across the top of the gland, and pick up oil and wax, which they then distribute over their feathers. While waterproofing is partly a result of feather structure, the constant coating of the feathers with the secretions of the uropygial gland is vital for survival in aquatic conditions.

The dipper, which at only seven to eight inches long is smaller than a robin, has a uropygial gland 10 times larger than those of other songbirds its size. Water instantly beads up and slides off the dipper's body as it emerges from a stream. In addition, like waterfowl, dippers have a thick coat of down beneath their outer contour feathers. And each time the bird dives, scale-like flaps automatically seal its nostrils.

The dipper is a solitary bird with a single-mindedness that is almost comical, especially when it rapidly dips its body up and down, perhaps for a better view of the area it is foraging. When the dipper is part of a mated pair, or when there are young fledglings, this dipping may also serve to communicate an individual's whereabouts to other family members. Dippers are closely related to the wrens and thrushes, and it is easy to see resemblances in the dipper's short, perky, wrenlike tail and its willingness to sing even in the coldest conditions. Indeed, the dipper is nonmigratory and stays on its home stream all winter, driven to lower altitudes only if the water freezes over.

Perhaps the most remarkable thing about this bird is its nest. Because we know just where to look for dippers, their nests, though well hidden, are relatively easy to find. We stand by a clear mountain river. It is May, breeding season. A dipper darts by, headed upstream, and disappears. We follow slowly along the shore, eyeing mounds of moss out in the water, watching for any irregularity of color or for the dipper itself to suddenly reappear, until we come to a steep-faced falls. Moss, ferns, and saxifrage compete for space within the range of the spray. Surely this spot is perfect for dippers. We sit down on a rock sheltered by willows and wait.

Which clump of moss could it be? All are equally green, like miniature gardens perpetually watered by the falls. The white stars on the long saxifrage stems bob with the impact of tiny drops as we wait, watching and musing. Could the dipper have passed up this classic nesting site for a less obvious spot? Suddenly she lands on the crest of the falls, an insect in her beak. She looks around and then drops straight down, momentarily disappearing behind the falls and reappearing on the other side to hang on the outside of a ball-shaped mound of moss. Gaping

yellow and orange beaks appear in a small hole in the moss. The insect is placed in one mouth and the female is off again, straight over the pool, headed back downstream. In five minutes she is back. Same pattern: top of the falls, look around, drop down, deliver, and straight out over the pool.

The nest itself is not actually a mound of growing moss but has been fashioned of pieces gathered by the female and interwoven to form an ovenlike structure that is kept green and fresh by the spray. Tucked behind the falls, the nest is utterly invisible

and inaccessible to the snakes, martens, weasels, minks, and raccoons that regularly patrol the shore, searching for eggs and young. When the nestlings defecate, their fecal sacs shoot several inches away from the nest before they drop and roll down a rock into the rushing water.

The female dipper has incubated the eggs, and now she does most of the food-gathering for her five nestlings. Dippers are polygynous; that is, the male may take more than one mate. Mated pairs often remain bonded for less than a month. Here in the mountains, the breeding season is short, and it is beneficial to the species for the male to get on with fathering a second brood. With her young protected in their cozy ball of moss, the female is free to forage alongshore and underwater, busily locating insects, especially the larvae of caddisflies and stoneflies that cling to the undersides of rocks. Plunging into even the swiftest channels, she keeps her head lowered as she walks, actually using the force of the water to stay submerged. In this way, she can maneuver in streams that would push us humans off our feet. Like a duck, though her feet are not webbed, the dipper may bob to the surface and paddle to shore, or she may fly straight out of the water with her food and land on a rock to eat. In shallower water she is more likely to submerge just her head, bracing herself against the swift current on feet that are larger, relative to her body size, than those of most songbirds. Like a swallow, the dipper can also catch insects in midair or scoop them off the surface of the water.

After 24 days in the nest, the young are ready to fledge. Although with their spotted breasts they rather resemble their thrush relatives, they leave the nest cleanly, with none of the ineptitude of most songbird young. These fledglings are more precocial, like waterfowl, and they can dive, swim, run, and even fly short distances without being taught. They remain only about a

Though dippers are songbirds, they are equally at home in the water and in the air. They fly through waterfalls, dive beneath the surface of the water, and reemerge, scarcely missing a wingbeat. With large oil glands and dense feathers, they repel the water the instant they surface.

week with their parents before departing to find watery territories of their own.

John Muir loved the dipper too. He wrote extensively about it as he roamed Yosemite with the bird as his companion. "One mild winter morning, when Yosemite Valley was swept its length from west to east by a cordial snowstorm, I sallied forth to see what I might learn and enjoy. A sort of gray, gloaming-like darkness filled the valley, the huge walls were out of sight, all ordinary sounds were smothered, and even the loudest booming of the falls was at times buried beneath the roar of the heavy-laden blast. The loose snow was already over five feet deep on the meadows, making extended walks impossible without the aid of snowshoes. I found no great difficulty, however, in making my way to a certain ripple on the river where one of my ouzels lived. He was at home, busily gleaning his breakfast among the pebbles of a shallow portion of the margin, apparently unaware of anything extraordinary in the weather. Presently he flew out to a stone against which the icy current was beating, and turning his back to the wind, sang as delightfully as a lark in springtime."

Dark-eyed Junco

One spring day I was out with some friends, planning the route for a new segment of trail through a small forested park within our town limits. As caretakers of the park, we had decided that one stretch of trail was too steep and slippery to be safe for some hikers, so we decided to route the trail off the spine of the ridge and, instead, bring it up a series of switchbacks on the west side. But huge Sitka spruce hung with lichen and moss, salal, and huckleberries made penetrating the underbrush difficult. The slope on either side of the trail was so steep and overgrown that we wound up widely separated, yelling to maintain contact.

After hours of stumbling over and under logs, skirting boulders, and falling into holes, we finally had a route marked with orange ribbons of surveyor's tape. But as we walked the course for a final check, from the sparse grass, a junco began scolding and then flew up from the ground. We looked at one another and groaned, realizing we must have routed the trail right past her nest. We marked with our eyes the point from which she darted, then walked over and parted the blades of grass to expose a tiny, moss-lined cup sunk in the forest duff, containing four bluish white eggs speckled with brown.

The female junco remained in a shrub close by, scolding us as we peeked at her eggs. We left her in peace and scrambled up the steep slope to the old trail. We stood there a moment and caught our breath, then headed once more out into the underbrush, orange ribbon in hand, down the opposite side of the ridge. Eventually, we got a new trail cut. Every time I walk it, I cast my eyes over toward the junco's slope and savor her privacy.

The dark-eyed junco is a widely distributed little sparrow well-known to people across the country who maintain bird feeders. For much of the year, the junco is predominantly a seed-

NEST
Cup of grass, moss, and twigs, usually built on the ground, often with overhead protection from vegetation

HABITAT
Forests

EGGS
3–6, white or pale blue with reddish brown markings

INCUBATION
12–13 days, by the female

BREEDING RANGE
Northern United States and Canada, much of the West

eater, but during the summer it catches insects to feed its young. While many cup nesters such as the robin often reveal the locations of their nests, flying straight to them with insects in their beaks, the junco secretively scratches in leaves on the ground and darts under the cover of low shrubs to the nest. At hatching, the reddish orange skin of the altricial nestlings is covered with a thin, dark gray down. When the mother returns to the nest, bright pink mouths rimmed with yellow pop open to receive food. On their protein-rich diet, the young mature quickly. The tarsi, or shanks of their legs, develop especially fast, an adaptation to ground nesting that enables the nestlings to flee on foot should a predator appear. In just nine to thirteen days the nestlings are ready to fly, though they remain dependent on their parents for three more weeks.

The odds for survival of a tiny, seemingly defenseless, four- to five-inch bird "camped out" for several weeks on the ground with its four or five fragile eggs, and later its blind and helpless young, at first glance seem impossibly low. But survival does not always go to the mighty, such as the Canada goose, or the loud and raucous, such as the terns. In fact, leaping to attack can be a fatal move for many small birds who, instead, rely on camouflage and even their diminutive size for protection. While the junco generally leaves its nest when threatened, scolding passersby with a characteristic *tuck, tuck,* many birds, such as the Kentucky warbler, the northern waterthrush, and the Wilson's warbler, simply stay put on the nest unless they are practically stepped on. The Wilson's warbler sits so tight that it gives the appearance of actually being tame, permitting stroking by a human hand and, if disturbed, often returning to the nest while the intruder is still close by. The ovenbird, while it makes its presence known with its reckless *teacher, teacher, teacher, teacher,* so characteristic of the eastern deciduous forests in springtime,

builds a nearly invisible little domed, ovenlike nest in which it stays put while on the eggs. I have often wondered how many times I may have placed my foot right on its doorstep as I walked Vermont woods in summer, the bird's little heart pounding as it watched, eye level with my boot.

For many people, these ground-nesting birds, who often spend their lives right in our midst, remain nothing more than a rustling in the leaves. But for the same reasons that modesty and understatement can be intriguing, many are drawn to these little birds, who live more like mice than eagles. As Uncle Remos says, ". . . and Bre'r Fox, he lay low," words I have often found to be a useful metaphor for survival.

Western Meadowlark

Imagine a dry, flat, windblown prairie. The grass seems to go on forever, just tall enough to bend in the wind, giving the prairie the fluid surface of a sea. An old fence post, remnant of a boundary long since abandoned, sticks out of the grass at an angle. The wire lies tangled under the grass, soon to be covered by yet another year's growth of vegetation. A bird flies in from the east and lands in the tall grass near the fence post. It does not hop but walks in and out of cover, its deliberate gait and flashing yellow plumage giving away just part of its identity. It is a meadowlark, but whether it is male or female, eastern or western species, is hard to determine. The sexes are nearly identical, and here in the center of the country, where the ranges of the two species overlap, it is thought that the birds themselves have trouble recognizing members of their own kind.

A second bird flies in, landing on the fence post and launching into a complex, flutelike, double-noted song. His rich song immediately identifies the male western meadowlark, *Sturnella neglecta*. John James Audubon gave it this species name because the bird was not distinguished as a separate species until 80 years after its eastern counterpart was first identified. From the fence post, the male proclaims his territory, while his mate continues walking off through the grass. While she appears to simply amble over the prairie, she actually follows a specific route, a narrow, bird-width path already beaten down by her feet. The grass leans over the path on both sides, creating a tunnel that shelters her from view. On the open prairie, it is imperative for survival that the nesting female not leave a trace of her presence but simply fade into the grass.

The meadowlark's nest, like the ovenbird's, is roofed like a little amphitheater. The female reaches it and disappears into the

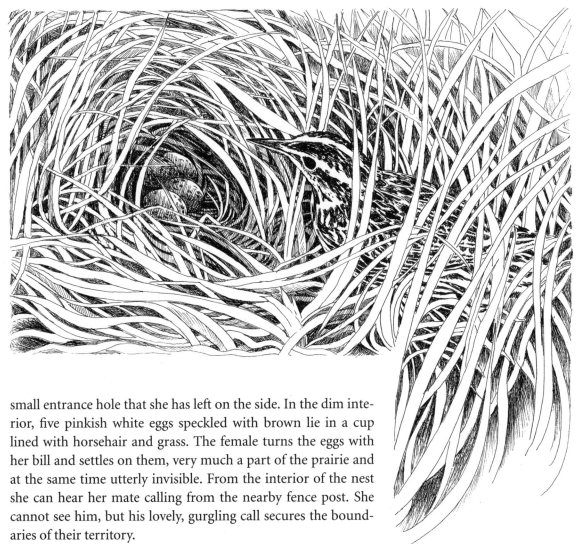

small entrance hole that she has left on the side. In the dim interior, five pinkish white eggs speckled with brown lie in a cup lined with horsehair and grass. The female turns the eggs with her bill and settles on them, very much a part of the prairie and at the same time utterly invisible. From the interior of the nest she can hear her mate calling from the nearby fence post. She cannot see him, but his lovely, gurgling call secures the boundaries of their territory.

The meadowlark is a grassland bird that benefited from the clearing of North America's vast deciduous forests, the ranges of the eastern and western species eventually coming together and overlapping on the central plains. Where the ranges of the two species overlap, it may be necessary to wait for the male to sing to tell them apart. Individual males of either species, however, may actually learn the calls of the other, making positive identification a challenge.

If you explore an area where a territorial male is singing, you may discover that there are several nests nearby. Sometimes these are multiple nests of a single female that have been left unfinished. Or a male may have more than one mate nesting in his territory; meadowlarks of both species tend to be polygynous. In addition, a female with young still in the nest may build a second nest and lay eggs while she and her mate are still feeding their first brood.

As with many songbirds, incubation lasts about two weeks, and the young are confined to the nest for another two weeks. The female builds the nest and completes incubation without the help of the male, but he shares in bringing insects to the five downy nestlings. By the eighth day, the exuberant nestlings begin to test the grass walls and roof of the nest. By the twelfth day they venture out into cover of the tall summer grass, eventually making short flights above the stalks of prairie wildflowers already going to seed.

Bobolink

A farmer gets an idea. It is early June in New England. He expects three or four days without rain, and he is in a hurry to get as much hay as possible cut and in the barn. But there is still time for ideas. Every year as he mows he sees bobolinks fly out of the grass, and he knows that he has cut over their nests, destroying the eggs. Now he thinks that it really wouldn't be that hard to get off the tractor when a bobolink flushes, locate the nest, and then cut around it. He feels good about his decision.

But finding the nests does not turn out to be easy. The farmer does not know that by the time a female flies up, she has already first walked a good distance away from the nest through the grass. The farmer steps carefully, staring down through the high grass, his determination building though he is losing precious time. He knows there is a nest. He does not want to get back on the tractor until he finds it. At last! He parts the grass with his arm, and there beneath him are the eggs, looking like six cinnamon-colored nuts, lying in a rough grass cup on the ground. He takes off his T-shirt, drapes it over the grass to mark the nest, and goes back to his idling tractor.

By the end of the morning his field looks a little silly, dotted with ragged tepees of grass that he has actually taken the time to tie up with baling twine. He reassures himself that his neighbors will not be looking at this back hayfield. Feeling proud and benevolent, he tells his wife about it when he goes in for lunch.

The next day he goes out to check the nests and make sure all is well. But no bobolink flushes as he approaches the first tepee. The farmer walks up and sees that the grass has been widely parted beneath the baling twine. He peers in the opening with dread and finds only pieces of brown-splotched eggshell, left by

NEST
Cup of coarse grasses lined with finer grasses, well concealed in dense grass
HABITAT
Most commonly in tall grass of hayfields, grain fields, meadows
EGGS
4–7, pale gray to cinnamon, heavily marked with brown
INCUBATION
10–13 days, by the female
BREEDING RANGE
Northern half of the United States

the skunk or raccoon that was attracted to the isolated teepees in the field of stubble. The farmer feels disappointment and irritation that one of the costs of haying is the loss of the bobolinks. Is he getting old, soft? It used to be that he didn't mind waging war against insects that were eating his fruits and vegetables, or woodchucks that mounded up soil in his hayfields, or raccoons that ate his corn. He walks to check the other two tepees and finds the scene of destruction just the same.

Bobolinks were once abundant throughout the northern half of the United States during the breeding season. When farming equipment was less efficient, haying was done later, after the weather was more reliable. Some farmers now postpone early hay cuts until the bobolinks have finished nesting, but most feel this delay is too expensive. Bobolinks' breeding season begins in mid- to late May; incubation lasts for 11 to 13 days; then the young remain in the nest for another two weeks. Even after that time, they are unable to fly for several days and remain dependent on their parents for food. A farmer who waited until he was certain there were no young boblinks in a field would lose more than a month of potential haying time. The most nutritious grass of the season is growing during this time, and it may be laid flat by heavy rain or go to seed with a resultant loss of food value. Additionally, as more farmers go out of business, there are fewer hayfields for bobolinks to nest in.

Bobolinks have become rare in much of their original breeding range. They raise only one brood per year, after which they tend to flock in marshy areas as blackbirds do. During migration, and in their winter range in Brazil and Argentina, they must contend with loss of habitat. Increasingly they are being replaced by their more common and adaptable relatives, the blackbirds, who bind their nests higher off the ground to sturdier grasses and shrubs.

Ruby-throated and Black-chinned Hummingbirds

Ruby-throated Hummingbird

NEST
Cup of plant down and fibers
attached to branch with spider
silk; outside covering of greenish
lichens; lined with plant down

HABITAT
Woods, gardens, orchards; often
over stream

EGGS
2, white

INCUBATION
11–14 days, by female

BREEDING RANGE
Eastern half of the United States
and southeastern Canada

Probably every person has a place, or a few places, where the spirit comes to rest and everyday realities seem irrelevant. An old friend of mine feels this way when he leaves his dentistry practice for a couple of weeks and sits in Nebraska corn stubble with his gun in his lap, waiting to shoot geese. I think the feeling such a place evokes is a sense of equilibrium between the outside world and the inner soul. There is no tension, no pressure, for once no need to make a change. For me, as I described in the introduction to this book, the egg room in the natural history museum in Santa Barbara is just such a place. It has been so since I first entered it over 20 years ago. There is even one particular nest to which I am drawn and before which I stand as if in front of a sacred object.

It is the nest of a black-chinned hummingbird, western counterpart of the well-known ruby-throated hummingbird. There are lots of hummingbird nests in the museum, all of them compact and intricate, but only one like this. This one is built right on top of an orange. Of course the original orange has been replaced by a very lifelike fake, so even though the nest was found in 1917, it remains unchanged year after year. When I look at this nest, with its "just-picked" orange, I like to imagine how it was built, and how it might have been found.

It is 1917, and the Santa Paula Valley, southeast of Santa Barbara, contains miles of continuous orange groves. This is condor country — home of the largest bird in North America as well as one of the smallest. Beyond the terrain that is suitable for cultivation, rugged mountains rise out of the valley, baked in the summer sun. But here in the lush valley floor it is time to pick the Valencias. Mexican workers are moving through the groves, climbing ladders, hauling big canvas picking bags up through dark, shiny leaves, avoiding fierce spines on the trunks.

Five feet off the ground in one of the trees, a female hummingbird sits within the tiny nest she built on top of an orange. She moves her needlelike beak back and forth, nervously watching the activity. Her nest has the consistency of a sponge, resilient, intricate, woven of plant down she has flown across the valley to gather from the river's sycamores and willows and interwoven with last year's thistledown. Bound with spider silk, the thick, rounded rim curves inward, cupping her body comfortingly, insulating her two eggs. The eggs are pure white, half an inch long, lying side by side, tucked warmly within the down of her breast.

Some of the workers carry their ladders, some drag them between trees. The sound of the dragging makes the little hummer tense further. A ladder is set up against the trunk of her tree. Time has taught all female hummingbirds an unconscious lesson — that they and their nests are virtually invisible. Even though this female has chosen an orange instead of a branch, she sits tight. The man sings as he ascends the ladder, picking the uppermost oranges first and working down. Last of all he circles the tree on foot, picking the oranges he can reach from the ground. Unnoticed, the little hummingbird darts out through the leaves just before the man's fingers close over her soft nest. He jerks his hand back instantly and peers in at the orange he was going to pick. He smiles and snips the stem above the nest. His boss's little daughter likes this sort of thing. He will save it for her.

Who knows what actually happened? It is, indeed, true that the nest was found in Sespe in 1917. And it is true that someone took the time to preserve the nest, to get it to the museum. I

Black-chinned Hummingbird
NEST
Cup of plant down woven with spider silk and covered with bits of leaves and flowers
HABITAT
Riparian woodland, chaparral, gardens, orange groves
EGGS
2, white
INCUBATION
13–16 days, by the female
BREEDING RANGE
Western states from Washington to Texas

Hummingbirds eat insects as well as nectar. In fact, they may have first begun eating nectar while visiting flowers in search of insects. Hummingbirds are now dependent on a high-energy diet. Humans with a similar metabolism would have to eat 285 pounds of hamburger every day.

hope it will be there for another hundred years, awing people with its ingenuity. I wonder how many people have stood before it just as I have, and, unknown to its finder, had their lives altered just a little. When I was a teenager I memorized a passage from an unpronounceable source of East Indian wisdom. It said, "What we have done will not be lost to all eternity. Everything ripens at its time and becomes fruit at its hour." How many times will this orange ripen? How many times will those eggs hatch in imaginations, years from now?

Fifteen species of hummingbird live within the boundaries of the United States. Before trying to understand many of the unique characteristics of this highly unusual and successful family, it helps to have in mind one word: nectar. While it is difficult to reconstruct the precise sequence of hummingbirds' evolution, the fact that nectar forms a major part of their diet has influenced nearly every other aspect of their lives. Originally insect eaters, perhaps related to the swifts, hummingbirds may have begun nectar feeding as they visited flowers in search of bugs. The hummingbirds may have begun drinking the sugar water as a source of liquid, but it eventually became the major part of their diet, though spiders and insects have remained an important source of protein. Hummingbirds' metabolism necessarily increased on this high-energy diet, a result well understood by anyone who has had to cope with "sugared-up" children. A person with a similar rate of metabolism would have to consume 285 pounds of hamburger a day to maintain a constant weight. Imagining how that person might acquire all that hamburger, without free access to a supermarket, helps to develop understanding for much of the urgency in a hummer's life. Because it is so small, it can go very little time without food before its body temperature begins to drop. As a result, the hummingbird has developed a sort of every-man-for-himself lifestyle in which

each bird remains solitary and highly defensive of its own territory for most of the year.

One important and often life-saving defense that has evolved in hummers is the ability to go into torpor, a sleeplike condition in which the hummingbird perches lifelessly on a branch, with its head dropped down on its chest and its feathers puffed out to conserve warmth. While a hummingbird normally has the highest body temperature of any bird, 105–109 degrees Fahrenheit, in a torpid state its body temperature may drop 30 degrees. And though its heart — the largest relative to body weight of any warm-blooded animal — has a normal resting rate of 250 beats per minute and the capacity to reach well over a thousand beats per minute during flight, during torpor the heart rate slows to approximately 50 beats per minute, and breathing becomes irregular. Torpor normally occurs when food shortages coincide with cold weather. A period of torpor lasts eight to fourteen hours, enough to get a hungry hummingbird through the night.

The ruby-throated hummingbird is the best-known of the North American species. While 14 species are concentrated in the western third of the country, the ruby-throat, the only hummingbird that nests east of the Mississippi River, occupies the other two thirds. When I lived in New England, I was always grateful when a ruby-throat suddenly appeared in my kitchen garden. I might have more fully appreciated that little bird had I known the lengths to which it went to get to Vermont. After wintering in southern Mexico and Central America, the ruby-throat, weighing 3 grams, or 1/10 the weight of a first-class letter, flies 500 to 600 miles across the Gulf of Mexico, nonstop. Before embarking on this crossing, the little bird stores up energy in minuscule layers of fat, increasing its body weight by 50 percent or more. Fishermen on the Gulf who have watched ruby-throats passing by their boats at sea have remarked that the birds flew by without even pausing to rest. One man reported seeing six in one day, flying about 25 feet off the water, headed north.

The ruby-throat times its arrival in the United States to coincide, often to the day, with the initial blossoming during March and April of many "hummingbird flowers" in the South. It then works its way north with the spring, generally not reaching Vermont until May. The male arrives first and stakes out a feeding territory over which he watches, dive-bombing intruders as he keeps an eye out for potential mates. When a female arrives, she chooses her own territory. Perhaps, considering these separatist tendencies and the birds' diminutive size, the male

A hummingbird nest holds the two nestlings closely when they are first hatched. Because it is flexible, however, it expands as they grow, finally becoming almost flat by the time the young are ready to fly.

hummingbird would never find a mate if he were dull in color or secretive. But with concave feathers specially adapted to catch the sun and reflect brilliant red-orange from his throat, he makes his presence known to competitors and females alike. At first, a female entering the male's territory is likely to be dive-bombed. But when she doesn't leave, the male begins other displays, wide arcs and short back-and-forth passes, until the male and female engage in an up-and-down display, facing one another at close range, and eventually copulate on the ground.

The tiny nest is often built over a brook on a drooping branch less than an inch in diameter. Only about an inch across and an inch high, even with the female inside, the nest is indistinguishable from other knots on the branch. The female hummingbird builds her nest from materials that sound almost fairylike: over a core of bud scales bound to the branch with spider silk, she tamps milkweed fluff, fern down, thistledown, and fireweed into a contoured lining. Unlike her western counterpart the black-chinned hummingbird, the ruby-throat covers the outside of her nest with gray-green lichens, which she binds into place with more spider silk and the web of tent caterpillars. It is a miniature masterpiece, a padded jewel box for two chalk white eggs no bigger than small beans.

Out of those two beautiful eggs hatch two of the most doubtful looking nestlings of the bird world. Apparently lifeless, and nearly naked, they look more like small caterpillars than birds, their slate-blue skin fringed with scant yellow down. Utterly blind, the tiny hatchlings lie with their heads tucked, their necks gruesomely thin and weak. Yet in just one and a half weeks they will be nearly as big as their mother. At first the female feeds them by inserting her tongue into their beaks and squirting nectar down their throats. As the nestlings grow, however, she begins regurgitating large quantities of insects and nectar from her

crop. It is hard to imagine how nestlings small enough to fit into a one-inch nest can withstand repeated thrusts of an inch-long needle down the throat. But the system works, and in about a month, the nestlings lift off the nest with a skill nearly equal to that of an adult.

Bee balm, jewelweed, bleeding-heart, columbine, honeysuckle; from flower to flower the little family moves, drinking nectar. This sweet substance is produced by flowers merely to attract pollinators. As hummingbirds drink, pollen grains, the male flowers' sex cells, are dusted onto their bills and heads in places just right to pollinate subsequent flowers' female sex organs. While bees are often guided to a flower by scent, birds have little sense of smell. As a result, flowers pollinated by hummingbirds, while showy, generally lack any fragrance. Many of these flowers, often tube-shaped and brightly colored, have evolved in exclusive interdependence with hummingbirds. The brilliant red trumpet flower is a classic example. While bees see this flower in shades of dark gray and, furthermore, are unable to reach its nectar because of its tube shape, the tiny hummingbird, with long beak and even longer tongue, is able to hover with ease as it literally laps the nectar up, moving its tongue at an astounding rate of 13 licks per second.

The breeding season lasts for most of the period of peak bloom, from March to July. During this time, the female may raise two and sometimes three broods, but she must have time, as well, to put on weight for the migration south. It amuses me to think of a 3-inch-long bird, much of which is beak, "putting on weight." Fat reserves gleaned from a diet of flower nectar and insects hardly sound "fat." Yet the ruby-throat and her offspring must double their weight before they can make the trip south, propelling themselves on 4-inch wingspans 500 miles over the ocean.

Red-eyed Vireo and
Brown-headed Cowbird

Red-eyed Vireo

NEST

Basketlike cup made of strips of
bark, grapevine, grasses, and
rootlets, suspended in the fork of
two twigs

HABITAT

Deciduous forest, mixed woods

EGGS

2–4, white with tiny brown or
black spots

INCUBATION

12–14 days, by the female

BREEDING RANGE

Northern tier and eastern half of
the United States; Canada

In the understory of saplings of a small woodlot of mixed deciduous trees, a firm cup nest hangs hammocklike in the fork of two small twigs. It is made of birch bark, strands of grapevine, stems of bindweed, and strips of the papery walls of a wasp's nest, festooned with green birch leaves and bound together with spider silk. Virtually invisible in her nest, a gray-green bird with bright red eyes intently watches the damp woods around her.

The nest of the red-eyed vireo seems clever, safe. Had it been supported more conventionally from below, it would have required a much wider branch, giving access to raccoons or opossums. But it is suspended from mere twigs, wrapped securely with a degree of craftsmanship that makes an observer stand, yet again, in awe of birds' precision and seeming clear intention. Yet the perfection of the nest is perhaps more impressive when viewed as a testimony to the concept of evolution. How many multitudes of nests were built over time, simple trial and error favoring the best builders, before this design was achieved?

There is nothing casual about the vireo's presence in this northeastern forest. This is no mourning dove, incubating on a simple platform of twigs after a winter spent in these same woods. The comparison is useful. The mourning dove, having expended no energy in travel and little in nest building and with a long breeding season at her disposal, may rear several broods. But the vireo has inherited a remarkably different fate. As a result, while mourning doves and other species favored by the settling of America flourish, the red-eyed vireo is one of many delicate jewels of the eastern and northern deciduous forests that are vanishing, unknown to most humans except serious birders.

Vireos, warblers, flycatchers, tanagers, and several of the thrushes are among the birds termed neotropical migrants. While we have long considered these birds "ours," they actually spend more months in the tropics than in the woods of the United States and Canada. In fact, two thirds of the species of birds that nest in the forests of the eastern United States and half of those that breed in the West, approximately 250 species of North American birds in all, are dependent for their continued existence on conditions largely beyond our control in politically troubled or poverty-stricken areas of Mexico, Central and South America, and islands of the Caribbean. On the heels of this realization rush in questions as to what threats our classic eastern summer birds might be facing each winter. The image of familiar birds, in the company of red-legged honeycreepeers or ruddy woodcreepers, fleeing smoldering tropical forest as it is cleared for sugar cane production, comes into my mind.

The vireo and other neotropical songbirds have it no easier when they leave their winter haunts. Picture a flock of birds, each of them weighing only ounces, beginning the long migration north from South America. They fly by night, refuel by day, but many of the feeding places along their accustomed route are gone, and they are unable to build up normal reserves of fat. When they reach the Gulf of Mexico, they face the hardest part of the journey: a 500-mile nonstop flight surrounded by nothing but darkness and stars and the open ocean. Landfall is not spirited. One writer describes standing on the beach of a barrier island off the Gulf Coast of Texas, watching songbirds plummet, emaciated and exhausted, into the low shrubs along the shore.

It is estimated that in the 20 years between 1960 and 1980,

Brown-headed Cowbird
NEST
Does not build a nest
HABITAT
Deciduous and coniferous woods; gardens, parks, agricultural areas
EGGS
4–5, white with brown speckles
INCUBATION
By host species
BREEDING RANGE
Throughout the United States; Canada

there may have been as much as a 50 percent drop in migrants, as indicated by the numbers appearing on Navy radar screens in the Gulf. The weakened condition of the surviving migrants underscores the importance of keeping critical "staging areas" along the migratory routes undeveloped. Wildlife refuges are not merely pleasant amenities, like parks set aside for human enjoyment; their locations often are strategically chosen by scientists who have carefully observed different species' minimum requirements for resting and refueling.

On yet another front, biologists have begun to realize that the demise of our songbirds may also be due to causes that lie closer to home. As we all know, development in this country has chopped up forests into increasingly smaller fragments. A road here, a subdivision there, a new house here, a shopping mall there — all of these have led to smaller parcels of woods and to an increasing amount of forest "margin." Now there is evidence that these small woodlots, precious to those who love wildlife, are actually dangerous and deceptive traps for many songbirds. Most of the predators that prey on small songbirds do not penetrate deep into large tracts of forests. Jays, crows, ravens, opossums, raccoons, house cats, dogs, gray squirrels, and skunks all prefer to stay to the edges of the forest. In an experiment in which fake nests containing quail eggs were placed in various types of forest conditions, the devastating impact of fragmentation was revealed. While 70 percent of the eggs were lost in small suburban woodlots, 48 percent were lost in larger rural woodlots. But only 2 percent were lost from nests put deep in uninterrupted tracts of forest in the Great Smoky Mountains National Park. It is hard to say which predator does the most damage. Some would say it is the blue jay, which robs nest after nest. Others would say the house cat. Which predator is most de-

The nest of the vireo is suspended, hammocklike, in the fork of two twigs. Generally these twigs would be far too small to support the nest if it were built in a more conventional manner, saddled over the top branch or lodged in the crotch of two branches. By constructing a sling, the vireos are able to nest at the very tips of the branches, where most predators cannot go.

structive depends in part on the location. But for downright caginess, it's hard to top the brown-headed cowbird.

In late April or early May, the male red-eyed vireo arrives in the woods a few days ahead of the female. He immediately begins exploring the woods, checking out potential territories. Once the female arrives, they narrow their claim to an area of a little more than an acre. The male periodically sings his defense from the treetops, while the female eyes the trees for appropriate forked branches anywhere from three to fifty feet off the ground.

She is drawn to inspect first one branch and then another, getting a feel for how her nest will be positioned and supported.

At last a location is chosen, midway up a sapling, 20 feet off the ground. The female flies to a grapevine and strips off a thin piece of bark, then returns to her chosen branch and begins building. Another bird is nearby, however, exploring the canopy for her own uses. Furtive, dodging, spying, with no nest material in her beak, the brown-headed cowbird watches the other birds in the forest.

Viewed objectively, the cowbird is a fascinating creature. Adapted for a nomadic life on the plains, where it followed herds of roaming bison, the cowbird sacrificed a settled home life for the open road. The cowbird was perhaps once a nest builder. Other members of its family, the Icteridae, are accomplished nest builders, especially the orioles, which create the most complex nests of any bird in North America. The cowbird, however, in its effort to keep up with traveling herds, may have begun straying too far from its own nest to make it back in time to lay its eggs. It began to deposit its eggs in other birds' nests, and eventually the instinct to construct a nest of its own was lost. The success of this system is evidenced by the massive flocks of cowbirds that have exploded onto the American scene in a relatively short time. While the cowbird was quite rare in colonial times, the clearing of American forests and the spread of agriculture have opened up unlimited opportunities.

After eyeing the songbirds in the area hard at work constructing their nests, the cowbird sets its sights on our pair of red-eyed vireos. She watches the female silently, unmoving, from 20 feet away, while the little vireo gathers strips of birch bark and lays them over the fork. They hang, twirling in the breeze, until she deftly binds them into a sling with grapevine and bindweed, wrapping and winding the supporting fibers.

The brown-headed cowbird is a native species that is remarkably adapted to wreak havoc on the lives of other songbirds. Originally a plains bird, it followed bison, hastily dropping its eggs in other birds' nests and moving on with the herd, while its eggs were incubated by the unsuspecting hosts.

Her mate periodically leaves off his singing to accompany her as she flies back and forth. The cowbird steals off unseen through the vegetation. By the end of the first day, the basic structure of the nest is visible.

The next day the cowbird is back again, watching the female thicken the walls and insulate them with grass and plant down. When the vireos leave momentarily, the cowbird flies to the nearly completed nest and peers inside. Simply by focusing on potential hosts, the cowbird synchronizes her own laying cycle. The female vireo refines the shape of the nest by climbing inside and trampling the grassy floor. As she works, her mate brings her a spider, a dragonfly, a grub, extending the food to her in his beak. The female takes the food with begging calls similar to those used by juveniles, quivering her wings. The nest is nearly complete. She adds a final coating of lichens to the outside and draws long threads of spider silk round and round, tucking in loose ends and polishing with her beak. Once the nest is finished, she crouches on a branch and raises her tail, uttering a *quotquot* call, encouraging the male to mate.

In a few days the first egg is laid. It is white with little gloss, sprinkled sparingly with dark brown speckles. The female will not begin incubation until the clutch is complete. She forages during the day and returns to the nest each morning to lay another egg. Meanwhile, the cowbird's hormones too are activated, her attention fixed on the elegant cup-shaped nest she perhaps views as her own. The vireo lays a third egg, and leaves. That afternoon, when the cowbird is sure the vireos are nowhere around, she flies to the nest, deftly punctures one of the eggs with her beak, and carries it off and eats it. The next morning she comes back while the vireos are away and lands near the nest, furtively looking around. Suddenly she darts to the nest, settles into it for about 20 seconds, and flies off. When the fe-

By watching a potential host bird, the cowbird synchronizes its own breeding cycle in order to be ready to lay an egg after it has removed one of its host's.

male vireo arrives, she settles, unsuspecting, on her own two eggs and the cowbird's egg and lays a fourth. She has been spending more and more time on the nest. Now, instead of flying away, she stays put. Her clutch of four eggs is complete, and she begins incubation.

Observing this change, the male takes up his post in the canopy. His song takes on a noticeable intensity, his broken phrases following one upon the other so fast he seems to be tripping over them. One series of notes is abruptly interrupted by another, the male seeming to abandon song after song with irritating consistency. But to the female vireo, the sound is perhaps soothing. The rushed pace of the song may not come so much from pure exuberance as from a need to maintain contact through the lush layers of growing leaves. While a female vireo on the nest is nearly impossible to locate visually, her mate's singing is a characteristic indicator of her presence nearby.

After about half an hour, the male suddenly stops. It is time for a break. The female, who has been utterly still, is instantly alert, looking around nervously. The male appears a moment later near the nest. Characteristically, now that the female is incubating, he no longer approaches the nest directly, but calls the female out with low, rasping notes. The female abruptly sails over the rim of the nest, heading straight for the male, and the two fly off through the canopy, the male in the lead. While the male forages, the female perches, preening, picking at bugs until the male returns with food for her. Each time he lands near her she begs, *tchet, tchet, tchet,* with quivering wings. After about seven or eight minutes, the female grows anxious to return to the nest and flies off. Entering secretively, she again sits motionless, while above, in the same tree as before, her mate resumes his nonstop half-phrases.

After 12 days, the female leaves the nest with half of a brown-speckled eggshell in her beak. The male notices instantly and leaves his singing perch to fly down to the nest. This time he approaches the nest and peers in. There he encounters the gaping, red-orange mouth of the newly hatched cowbird. Its body is naked except for thin gray down, and its dark eyes bulge behind transparent lids. The male immediately flies off and in moments returns with a grub. The female is back on the nest, and he passes the food to her. She, in turn, feeds it to the cowbird.

Over the next several days, the three vireo eggs in the nest hatch. In other nests nearby in the forest, four biological siblings

Some birds will throw out a
cowbird egg or build a new floor
over the bottom of the nest, as in
this cross section of a yellow
warbler nest.

of the cowbird nestling hatch as well. In the nests of a redstart, a veery, another red-eyed vireo, and a yellow warbler, one egg was laid each day. The choice of hosts was not random. Certain characteristics make a bird eligible to serve as a cowbird host: Its eggs must be approximately the same size as those of the cowbird, its young must be fed a suitable diet of insects, and the young must be fed for at least two weeks after leaving the nest. A bird with precocial young, such as the killdeer, is a disastrous foster parent. Cowbird nestlings have been found dead in killdeer nests, obviously abandoned as soon as the precocial killdeer chicks were dry. Even a bird such as a swallow, though it has altricial young, does not qualify as a host because its young are taught to catch insects on the wing shortly after fledging. A dove, which feeds its young with "pigeon milk," would be an inappropriate choice, as would a kingfisher, which at first regurgitates fish and later delivers them whole. A cowbird egg was once found in a hummingbird nest, but it completely filled the inside cavity, and the nest was abandoned.

While there are at least 150 species of songbirds that could be suitable cowbird hosts, some eligible birds such as the robin and the catbird are simply intolerant of cowbird eggs in their nests and throw them out almost without fail. The yellow warbler has become well known for its interesting approach to the problem. Upon discovering a cowbird egg, it simply builds a new nest over its old one, burying its own eggs along with that of the cowbird, and begins a new family. Yellow warbler nests have been found six or more floors deep, with eggs sandwiched between each level. Other species occasionally adopt this approach as well, but of course, it is an expensive solution, costing the host precious time and energy.

The nestling cowbird grows noticeably faster than the nestling red-eyed vireos, doubling its weight in each of the first two days of its life. It is the cowbird's beak, gaping uppermost and widest, that the adults see first when they return with food. Each female cowbird generally defends a defined territory and lays one egg in each host nest. But in the absence of enough victims, territories may begin to overlap. Under these conditions, more than one cowbird may lay its egg in a host nest, and the resulting large and aggressive nestlings often overwhelm those of the host. Nests have been found where the host incubated four cowbird eggs and none of its own. After the cowbird lays its first "clutch" of about five eggs, it rests for a few days and then begins another clutch. With no family responsibilities, it is obvious why reproductive potential for the species is so high. It is estimated that each female is capable of producing 40 eggs each season.

As human overpopulation continues to grow, and the diversity of species on our planet continues to decrease, one could argue that it is fortunate that there are resilient species such as cowbirds, jays, crows, and starlings to take over. While I am not yet resigned to giving up warblers and vireos and tanagers, the day may come when we'll be glad to see any bird at all in the sky.

8

Pendulous Nests

~

If I were asked to choose which kind of baby bird I would like to be, I would not put myself deep in the earth sitting on a pile of fish bones with the kingfisher nestlings. And I would not sit on a cold cliff out at sea, no matter how thick my down might be. And I certainly would not fight it out in a heron nest or snuggle into rotting mouse remains with my fellow barn owlets. For my avian mother, I would pick a bird that lays her eggs in a pendulous nest, so that from the moment I was hatched, I would be swinging in the breeze in a soft, warm pouch with relatively benign siblings.

The northern oriole's tightly woven pouch is suspended from fine twigs, out of reach of predators.

Northern Oriole

NEST
Suspended pouch woven of plant
fibers, bark, yarn, and hair, lined
with cottony plant fibers
HABITAT
Deciduous woodlands, open areas
with scattered trees, orchards
EGGS
4–5, white with brown scrawls
and blotches
INCUBATION
12–14 days, by the female
BREEDING RANGE
Throughout the United States

A book on nests must end with the orioles. The evolution of birds and nests is a journey upward and outward — up trees and out on ever-smaller twigs — and the oriole represents the ultimate extension of that movement. A nearly robin-sized bird, it manages to nest as close to thin air as any bird can.

High above the ground in a clump of maple leaves at the end of a branch, the nest is invisible from below. But the female, flying to it with pieces of string and grass, plant fiber, grapevine bark, and horsehair, gives away its general location. For almost a week she comes and goes, weaving first one wall and then a second, finally joining them into an elongated pouch. After the fact, it is hard to imagine how one bird could have woven such a nest without blueprints, much less without premeditation. The fibers appear to be precisely twined and deliberately knotted, but in fact the process is not quite that fussy. As she builds, the female oriole moves her head with a rapid shuttling motion, tangling nesting material with her beak and then pushing it into shape like felted wool.

Young orioles in the nest are remarkably quiet. Swinging in the wind at the tip of a long branch perhaps 40, even 50 feet off the ground, the breeze scarcely penetrates the secure walls. On a bed of fine grasses, wool, hair, and cottony fibers, the nestlings rock gently back and forth. I can't think of a safer or more comfortable refuge.

While the habits of the oriole during breeding season are generally similar to those of most other North American passerines, its bright color and complex nest help us perceive it as the tropical bird it truly is. A well-known ornithologist, Alexander Skutch, wrote about the oriole's life from his home in Costa Rica. He suggested that a typical oriole might well live most of each year in just two trees, the orange tree outside his window in winter and an elm in New England in which it might construct its nest in summer. Unfortunately, the oriole's winter tree is just as likely to be in a mature tropical forest vulnerable to deforestation. Here on the other side of the equator, most of the elms that so beautifully supported oriole nests at the tips of their graceful branches have died. But in the oriole's favor is the design of its pouchlike nest, which offers excellent protection from jays and most other North American predators.

For those who listen each year for the return of the orioles, an event that often occurs on the very day the apple blossoms open, the season is not complete until the male's bold song suddenly intrudes on the sounds of spring. At the end of our barnyard in Vermont there was a maple — a particular branch, in fact — to which a male northern oriole returned each spring, a few days ahead of his mate. I would stand searching the yellow-green leaves, knowing from past experience just where to look, yet each year I was shocked by the bold appearance of the gleaming bird, fresh from the tropics, belting out his song to New England. The red-orange of a male oriole's feathers, after the drabness of winter, is as shocking as if a large goldfish were in the tree. His song, uttered with absolutely no warm-up, throws the season into forward gear in a moment, guaranteeing summer.

* * *

Writing this book has been a journey for me, a journey through evolution. Beginning with the ground nesters, observing as birds began to pick up sticks, watching as they began to elevate those sticks and then weave them together, has been a trip full of surprises. These surprises have increasingly made me a slave to fact. The facts are humbling. Like the characters in a mystery story, they have pushed me aside and gained a life of their own.

Yet because they are true, because orioles are actually out there, and vireos, and hummingbirds, I have found the facts more exciting than the elements of any mystery story I might have invented.

Yet now that I have completed this evolutionary journey, I know that the ground nesters are equal in wonder to any bird. Anyone who has watched gannets on a sunny afternoon, their bodies creamy white against a bright blue sky as they pause to aim before plummeting headfirst into the Atlantic, knows that their elegance is unsurpassed. When I am sitting low in the water in my kayak in the delta of the Eel River, with cormorants flying over, dropping white banners of excrement onto the cottonwoods nearby, their wings whistling as they power themselves up and down the river in abundant numbers, I want to say, like a politician with outstretched arms, "I love you all." My kids think I'm crazy. No, actually, I guess they don't. They know me well enough that I don't have to explain.

I just know that when a tiny rufous hummingbird pushes into my yard, fueling up for the second half of a 2,500-mile migration north, I am suddenly her straight-faced servant. What can I write that will help protect her? Will there be nectar-rich flowers available in backyards along her route? Will she be safe from poisonous sprays? I wonder, where is the tiny branch on which she will lay down willow seed and moss, and bind it with spider web and camouflage it with bits of bark? What five or six leaves will shade her? I watch her gulp sugar water, the muscles of her throat moving, and just hope she will find her destination safe when she arrives.